ALASKA'S GLACIER BAY

A TRAVELER'S GUIDE

KAREN JETTMAR

D0612567

Alaska Northwest Books™
Anchorage • Seattle • Portland

*To my parents, especially my mom, who heard the white
thunder with me in Muir Inlet*

Acknowledgments: I thank the many companions who've explored
Glacier Bay country with me, seeking the wilderness within and
around us. Thanks to S. Edwards, K. Ashton, M. Gladziszewski, C.
Gabriele, M. Heacox, R. Yerxa for manuscript review, and to M.
Steiert, and C. Summers for technical assistance. To the Tlingit of
Hoonah, especially the Huna Traditional Council of Elders, and Amy
Marvin, *Naa Tlaa* (Clan Mother) of the Chookaneidí, *gunalchéesh*
(thank you). Finally, I honor *Sit´ tu ḵwáani*, the glacier spirits, and *Ca tu
ḵwáani*, the mountain spirits, in whose presence I am eternally in awe.

Disclaimer: The discussions in this book on trip activities and edible
wild foods available in Glacier Bay are intended as information only.
Neither the author nor the publisher is responsible for any adverse
results individuals might experience from undertaking trip activities
or from eating wild foods.

Library of Congress Cataloging-in-Publication Data
Jettmar, Karen, 1951–
    Alaska's Glacier Bay : a traveler's guide / Karen Jettmar.
      p.   cm.
    ISBN 0-88240-486-5
    1. Glacier Bay (Alaska)--Guidebooks.   I. Title.
F912.G5J48   1997
917.98'2--DC21   97-4257
                                        CIP

Originating Editor: Marlene Blessing; Managing Editor: Ellen
Harkins Wheat; Editor: Linda Gunnarson; Designer: Cameron
Mason; Map: Gray Mouse Graphics.

Photographs: All photographs are by Karen Jettmar, except: Front
cover, pp. 3, 9, 10, 37, 52, 56, 84, 91, Clarence Summers; p. 62, E.M.
Kindle #100, U.S. Geological Survey; p. 65, #NA2094, and p. 68,
Partridge #7964, Special Collections Division, University of
Washington Libraries; p. 70, H.F. Reid #222, 1890, and p. 72, Winter
& Pond #168, W.O. Field Collection, Alaska & Polar Regions Dept.,
University of Alaska Fairbanks.

Alaska Northwest Books™
An imprint of Graphic Arts Center Publishing Company
Editorial office: 2208 NW Market St., Suite 300, Seattle, WA 98107
Catalog and order dept.: P.O. Box 10306, Portland, OR 97210
Telephone: 1-800-452-3032

Printed in the United States of America

CONTENTS

INTRODUCTION

GLACIER BAY,
A LANDSCAPE IN MOTION

GLACIERS MOVE IN TIDES. SO DO MOUNTAINS,
SO DO ALL THINGS.
—John Muir, *John of the Mountains* (1872)

When Captain George Vancouver sailed the waters of Icy Strait more than two centuries ago, Glacier Bay was a tiny recess a few miles deep "terminated by compact solid mountains of ice rising perpendicularly from the water's edge." Today, Glacier Bay is a deepwater fjord system with 2 arms, Muir Inlet and the West Arm, each nearly 65 miles long. Where a 4,000- to 5,000-foot-thick ice sheet existed, geologically speaking, just a moment ago in time, is now a living, vibrant bay. In Glacier Bay, rivers of ice spill off a score of peaks in excess of 10,000 feet, dropping huge icebergs into the sea, forming one of the largest concentrations of tidewater glaciers in the world. Amidst desolate landscapes created by the fastest glacial retreat ever recorded, we find austere beauty, and we observe life returning to the land, to carpet its contours and fill its waters with fish, its forest with animals, its skies with the sound of birds.

◄ THE FAIRWEATHER MOUNTAINS SHINE IN THE DISTANCE, TOWERING ABOVE BRADY GLACIER.

Like many of you, I first ventured to Alaska as a visitor to experience wilderness and see wildlife. I saw Glacier Bay for the first time 24 years ago. Fresh out of college in 1973, I flew from Maryland to

Anchorage and spent 2 months traveling around the state, eventually making my way to the docks of Juneau. I was on my way to see the place I'd heard so much about from a friend, who was spending his second summer season working as a park ranger at Glacier Bay. I hitched a ride aboard a 50-foot fishing boat crewed by 7 rowdy fishermen. It was late evening when we tied up at the dock in Bartlett Cove. I hopped aboard my friend's boat and we motored up Muir Inlet to Goose Cove, where he was stationed in the backcountry. In the darkness, I was only vaguely aware of the distance we were traveling, and the expanse of water, ice, and rock that surrounded us.

Several hours later, we pulled up alongside two 10-by-12-foot wall tents atop floating rafts just inside the cove—the Goose Cove Ranger Station. Tucked into one of the tiny bunks, I drifted off to sleep to the sounds of water lapping against the hollow metal floats. The next morning, stepping outside the wall tent, I found myself amid an austere landscape. On the shore were huge crystalline icebergs, stranded by the tide. Beyond the mouth of the cove, ice floated by. The land around me was open, a chaos of rock rubble, with scattered low alder bushes and mountain vistas all around. I marveled at the massive glaciated peaks, polished granite fjords, and aquamarine ice sculptures. In the days following, while my ranger friends patrolled the park, I rowed a small dory out of Goose Cove to Sealers Island and sat for hours on scoured bedrock, watching and listening, as icebergs moved continuously by, except when the magic moment of slack tide arrived and everything seemed to stand still; then, I was surrounded by a profound silence, save the popping and cracking of ice and the distant thunder of calving glaciers.

Though I arrived at Glacier Bay a nanosecond ago in geologic time, I have seen dramatic change. Two decades ago, I hiked all over upper Muir Inlet, from Muir Point north. Glacial barrens with scattered plant life covered hundreds of square miles. Today, the land is covered with near-impenetrable alder–willow thickets. Muir Glacier calved ice constantly then, and the inlet was often choked with icebergs. Today, Muir is backing up onto dry land, and its terminus barely extends into tidewater. McBride Glacier was still an ice front extending into Muir Inlet.

Now, its face has shrunk back, forming a huge ▲ THE AUTHOR
embayment and revealing new land; a new PADDLES
fjord has formed in just 20 years—a fraction of THROUGH
a lifetime. When I first saw Wachusett Inlet, UPPER MUIR
INLET.
ice fell from Plateau Glacier into tidewater,
leaving a lapis lazuli pocket in the face of the glacier. Now,
the glacier is gone, completely melted. Kayakers used to
paddle freely through Hugh Miller Inlet, into Scidmore
Bay, and back out into the West Arm. Now we carry our
kayaks over a gravel beach. The land is rising, freed from
the weight of ancient ice.

A landscape in motion, Glacier Bay National Park and
Preserve is still emerging from the Ice Age. Here, change
is occurring so rapidly that we can observe geological
forces reshaping the land at every moment. Come feast
your senses on what some call the most spectacular fjord
system in the world. Here, in an area of 5,100 square miles,
lie mountain ranges, glaciers that have never known the
imprint of a human foot, streams, rivers, meadows, forests,
wetlands, and arms of the sea still undergoing formation.
See it for what it is—a work of art in progress. Come back
next week, or next year, or a decade from now, and it will
be different. The artist is still sculpting this work.

As a trip planner and basic guide to the park, this book provides you with facts about Glacier Bay's fascinating natural history, as well as detailed travel information to help you get the most from your visit. The first chapter provides basic visitor information in compact form: facts about the park, details on logistics and accommodations, and suggested ways to explore the park. Next comes a chapter on glaciers, the ice age architects of this magnificent landscape. The following chapter explains how plants have come to reinhabit the glacial landscape and describes the diversity of flora at Glacier Bay. Chapters on wildlife provide information about wondrous mammals, birds, insects, whales, seals, sea otters, and more. From here you'll move on to learn about the early Tlingit inhabitants of Glacier Bay and their sacred ties to the landscape, and about John Muir's influences on conservation, tourism, and scientific research in the park. Two later chapters take you outside Glacier Bay proper: one visits the outer coast, a remote region of the park encompassing headlands, bays, and beaches along the Gulf of Alaska; the second explores the Tatshenshini and Alsek Rivers and Glacier Bay National Preserve. The final chapter describes Gustavus, the small community that serves as a gateway to the park. With this guide as your companion, I hope you'll take time to experience the wildness of Glacier Bay National Park and Preserve and make your own personal discoveries—however small or large—in this immense landscape. I also hope you'll do what you can to support protection of the world's wild places.

▶ GLACIALLY SCOURED BEDROCK IN RENDU INLET.
▼ MELTWATER POURS FROM ICE CAVE.

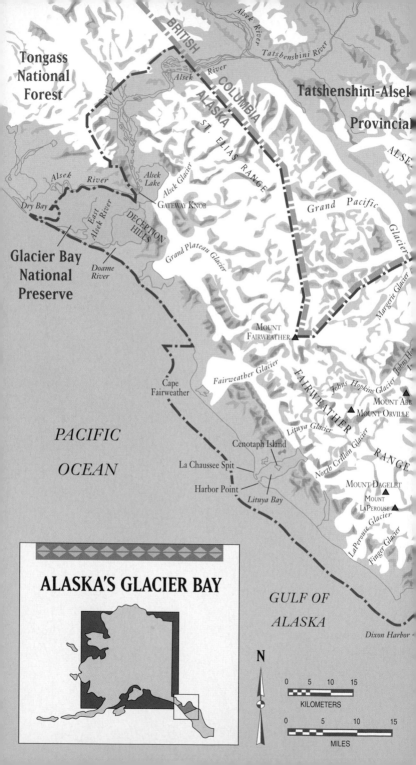

AT A GLANCE

GLACIER BAY NATIONAL
PARK AND PRESERVE

Glacier Bay National Park and Preserve was originally established as a national monument in 1925 to protect the glacial environment and plant communities for public enjoyment, scientific study, and historic interest. It was enlarged to add marine waters in 1939; Gustavus was removed in 1955; and then the area was enlarged again in 1978. With passage of the Alaska National Interest Lands Conservation Act in 1980, Glacier Bay became a national park and was enlarged to the northwest by 585,000 acres, including a national preserve of 55,000 acres, set aside to protect fish and wildlife habitat and migration routes along the Alsek River.

In 1986, the United Nations Educational, Scientific, and Cultural Organization (UNESCO) established the Glacier Bay–Admiralty Island Biosphere Reserve, recognizing the importance of protecting the region's biodiversity. In 1992, UNESCO designated Glacier Bay a World Heritage Site, part of the existing Wrangell– St. Elias–Kluane National Parks World Heritage Site, the principal international recognition given to natural and cultural areas of universal significance.

◄ MARGERIE GLACIER TOWERS ABOVE A TOURBOAT IN TARR INLET.

SIZE: 3,280,000 acres. About 80 percent, or 2,659,876 acres of park lands and waters, are federally designated wilderness under the Wilderness Act. Wilderness waters exist in Rendu, Hugh Miller, and Adams Inlets; in the north and west arms of Dundas Bay; and surrounding the Beardslee Islands. Glacier Bay contains the largest protected marine sanctuary in the world.

LOCATION/ACCESS: Glacier Bay is located in Southeast Alaska, about 70 miles northwest of Juneau and 600 miles southeast of Anchorage. There is no road access into the park. Regularly scheduled air service to Gustavus is available from Juneau, Haines, Yakutat, and Skagway. A single road links Gustavus airport with the park, 10 miles distant. Bus and taxi service are available. Cruise ships enter Glacier Bay but do not drop off people in the park. Seasonal boat service is available from Juneau to Gustavus dock. Private boats may enter Glacier Bay with a permit. No dock space is available for private vessels, but safe anchorage exists in Bartlett Cove. Floatplanes may land in park waters with a permit; a floatplane dock exists in Bartlett Cove for temporary activities.

HIGH POINT: 15,320-foot Mount Fairweather.

USGS MAPS: Juneau, Mount Fairweather, Skagway, Yakutat; also a special USGS topo map of Glacier Bay; NOAA charts 17300 and 17318.

SEASON: Open year-round, but few winter services.

FEES: No entrance fees are charged.

LODGING AND FOOD: Glacier Bay Lodge, inside the park, is open from mid-May to mid-September; 56 regular hotel rooms and hostel-style bunk-bed lodging are available, with a full-service restaurant and bar. Several inns, cafes, and many bed-and-breakfasts are in Gustavus. Inns in Gustavus serve dinner to nonguests by reservation. There's a small grocery/variety store in Gustavus.

GAS: No. 2 diesel, unleaded gas, and white gas are available at Bartlett Cove dock. Jet–A, avgas, and gasoline are available in Gustavus.

ACCESS FOR PHYSICALLY CHALLENGED: There is a ramp entry to Glacier Bay Lodge and rooms. The tour boat has a ramp.

VISITOR CENTER/INTERPRETIVE PROGRAMS: The visitor center, with information desk, theater, and exhibits is located upstairs (mezzanine level) in Glacier Bay Lodge. Park naturalists lead morning trail walks and host audiovisual presentations in the theater each evening. On tour boats

WHERE'S THE FAIR WEATHER?

The grandeur of Glacier Bay was created by water. With a maritime climate, fog and overcast skies are more common than sunshine. Rain creates and perpetuates glaciers and rain forests—there's up to 125 inches of it on the bay, with an average of 75 inches annually, including 14 feet of snow. Gustavus receives less—55 to 60 inches of rain per year. Summer daytime temperatures in the lower bay average in the 50s and 60s; nights are cooler. Upper Glacier Bay can be as much as 15 degrees cooler, due to the presence of glaciers. The outer coast has milder temperatures and more precipitation, but less snowfall due to the Japanese Current's influence. In the Fairweather Range, storms coming off the Pacific Ocean linger in the peaks, dropping some 180 inches of precipitation, much of it in the form of snow during fall and winter months, sustaining extensive glacial systems.

Anyone who has spent any length of time at Glacier Bay quickly becomes familiar with its weather. Studying the glaciers in 1892, geologist Harry F. Reid watched a steady rainfall from his tent on a shore of Geikie Inlet and observed wryly in his field journal: "We have concluded that there are many infallible signs of rain in this region. If the sun shines, if the stars appear, if there are clouds or if there are none; these are all sure indications. If the barometer falls it will rain; if the barometer rises, it will rain; if the barometer remains steady, it will continue to rain."

The weather is driest in spring and early summer, during April, May, and June. September and October are generally the wettest months, but there can be spectacularly clear days any time of the year, as well as rainfall anytime. Dress appropriately, with a few layers of wool or synthetic pile, a windproof shell and full-protection rain gear, a hat, waterproof boots, sunscreen, and insect repellent, and you'll be ready to enjoy Glacier Bay, whether it's drizzling in mist or dazzling in sunlight.

and cruise ships in Glacier Bay, onboard park naturalists provide natural history narration. Glacier Bay publications, maps, and charts are for sale at the visitor center.

PETS: Pets are permitted on leash in Bartlett Cove, but must be kept aboard vessels anywhere else in the park.

BIRD-WATCHING: More than 220 bird species.

BOAT TOURS: To see tidewater glaciers (the nearest one is 45 miles from Bartlett Cove), you must travel up-bay. A 9-hour boat trip up Glacier Bay and West Arm, with a park naturalist on board, is available through Glacier Bay Lodge and other boat charters.

PRIVATE BOATING: Permits are required from May 1 through August 31 for motorized private boats. Permits run from midnight to midnight for a maximum of 7 days in July or 14 days during May, June, August, and September; permits are limited to 25 boats at one time. Applications cannot be mailed more than 60 days before your requested date of arrival in the park. Adams, Hugh Miller, Charpentier, and Rendu Inlets and waters in the Beardslee Islands are motorless wilderness waters; as such, they are closed to powerboats and floatplane landings from May 1 through September 15. Muir Inlet is closed to motorboats from June 1 through July 15; Wachusett Inlet

▼ KAYAKERS ARE DROPPED OFF ON SEBREE ISLAND.
is closed to motorboats from July 16 through August 31.

CRUISE SHIP TOURS: Cruises up the Inside Passage often include a stop at Glacier Bay.

For a list of cruise ship companies that tour the bay, write to the park.

FISHING: An Alaska fishing license is required for all fishing. License available at Glacier Bay Lodge and in Gustavus. Halibut, salmon, Dolly Varden, and cutthroat trout are sought-after species. Half- to 1-day fishing tours are offered through local charters in Gustavus.

HIKING: There are only 3 hiking trails in the park. All are in the Bartlett Cove area. One-mile Forest Trail begins at Glacier Bay Lodge, winds through spruce–hemlock forest, and descends to the beach. Bartlett River Trail, 5 miles round-trip, begins on the park road about a mile east of the lodge, meanders along a tidal lagoon and through the rain forest, then emerges and ends on the Bartlett River estuary. Bartlett Lake Trail branches off a half mile down the Bartlett River Trail, reaching the lake, 4 miles later (9 miles round-trip). Other hiking possibilities are along the beach, from Bartlett Cove dock to Point Gustavus (7 miles one way), around Point Gustavus to Gustavus (14 miles one way), and the back roads and beaches of Gustavus. Trail maps are available from the Park Service.

CAMPING/BACKPACKING: Camping in the park is allowed by registration/permit only. The Park Service maintains a free campground at Bartlett Cove that is open year-round; there are about 35 campsites, first come, first served, with a 14-day limit. A bear-resistant food cache, gear storage shed, fire pits, and firewood are available. Fires are permitted only in designated areas. Camping is allowed anywhere in the backcountry, except on closed islands, but cross-country hiking can be extremely challenging in many areas due to dense brush and glacial streams. Check with the Backcountry Office (located near Bartlett Cove dock) for current regulations and restricted areas. Park rangers offer twice-daily (mandatory) backcountry orientation for all multiday hikers and kayakers. Popular kayaking areas allow limited numbers, to avoid overcrowding. Check with the Park Service prior to arrival to plan your itinerary. In the backcountry, portable stoves are necessary and all food must be carried in bearproof cannisters provided by the park. Shower and laundromat are available at Glacier Bay Lodge.

KAYAKING: A great way to see the park, but not

BEING A RESPECTFUL VISITOR

◆ As in all national parks, please leave plants, animals, fossils, interglacial wood (freeze-dried remnants of ancient forest), and shells as you found them for everyone to enjoy, now and in the next generation. Destroying or defacing natural features is prohibited, as is feeding, capturing, molesting, or killing any animal in the park.

◆ Give wildlife plenty of space. Observe all wildlife from a safe distance so as not to disturb them (at least 100 yards). Be respectful of rookeries and nesting and denning areas. Stay clear of beaches where flightless molting geese, loons, and scoters are gathered. Stay off islands with bird rookeries. Use binoculars and take photos using a telephoto lens.

◆ Do not pursue any marine mammal or bird in a boat or kayak. Maintain a distance of at least 100 yards between your watercraft and wildlife. If your presence is changing wildlife behavior, then you're too close.

◆ Stay on designated trails; where there are no trails, do low-impact hiking by walking on the most durable surfaces (hard sand, rock, gravel).

◆ When camping, cook and eat below the high-tide line, and camp out of sight and away from wildlife travel routes on sites that lack vegetation. Avoid camping on fragile vegetation, such as wildflower meadows. When hiking in pristine areas, spread out to avoid making traffic routes where vegetation is present. In established high-use areas, place tents on sites that are highly impacted.

◆ Protect wildlife, particularly bears, by storing your food properly. Once bears become habituated to humans, they may become aggressive "problem" bears.

◆ Respect wildlife by leaving your pets at home.

◆ Respect other visitors' needs for solitude.

◆ Treat all water as precious; camp away from freshwater sources to avoid contamination.

◆ Pack out all your trash and garbage.

◆ Avoid the use of campfires in the backcountry.

recommended for novices. Boat service from Juneau will carry kayaks to Gustavus. There are kayak rentals and guided tours available in Bartlett Cove. Lodge tour boat provides back-packer/kayaker drop-off service for a fee.

▲ HIKERS IN THE ALSEK RIVER VALLEY EXPERIENCE THE DRAMA OF GLACIERS CLOSE-UP.

MOUNTAINEERING: The Fairweather Mountains offer challenging climbing, due to remoteness, height of peaks, difficult access, severe weather, and glacial conditions. Specialized equipment, expedition experience, and permits are required. Most climbs are made between March and May, when the snow is firm.

RIVER RAFTING: A permit is required to run the Tatshenshini and Alsek Rivers; there is an annual lottery. Ten-day guided trips are available from June through September. Contact the park for list of operators.

HUNTING: Prohibited in the park, except in Glacier Bay National Preserve with an Alaska hunting license; consult Alaska Department of Fish and Game for regulations. Firearm possession is prohibited at Glacier Bay, except in the preserve and northwest "panhandle" of the park.

SCENIC FLIGHTS: Air tours of the park and charters, including floatplane service, may be arranged in Juneau, Haines, Yakutat, and Gustavus, or at Glacier Bay Lodge.

FOR MORE INFORMATION: Write or call the Superintendent, Glacier Bay National Park and Preserve, P.O. Box 140, Gustavus, AK 99826; (907) 697-2230. Maps, marine charts, and books may be purchased through the Alaska Natural History Association, Gustavus, AK 99826.

GLACIERS, ICE AGE ARCHITECTS

We saw the world-shaping forces at work," wrote ornithologist John Burroughs upon visiting Glacier Bay for the first time in 1899. "We saw them transport enormous rocks, and tons and tons of soil and debris from the distant mountains. . . . We witnessed the formation of the low mounds and ridges and bowl-shaped depressions that so often diversify our landscapes— all the while with the muffled thunder of the falling bergs in our ears." Unique in the world for its many rivers of ice tumbling into the sea, Glacier Bay is a living laboratory of glacial geology. Here, you can see how glaciers have chiseled the land into U-shaped valleys and sculpted the peaks, leaving behind moraines or pushing them into the sea.

I'm sitting in my kayak in Johns Hopkins Inlet, paddling slowly along the north shore of a sheer-sided cathedral of rock and ice. Smooth rock walls are deeply grooved, evidence of the glacier that once stood where I'm floating. Before me, the fjord is covered with glittering icebergs. Each berg is a unique sculpture, reminding me of something living—a graceful swan, an imposing walrus, a gossamer tern. Dancing in the sunlight, their ephemeral beauty is mine alone, for they melt before my eyes. I think about the paradox of ice in nature. Delicate, transparent, chameleon-like, ice changes from lacy snowflakes to an undulating

◄ TOPEKA GLACIER SCOURS A U-SHAPED VALLEY AS IT ADVANCES TO JOHNS HOPKINS INLET.

frozen river, tearing at mountainsides and crushing all in its path.

Nearly surrounding me, 7 glaciers tumble into the sea; others cling precariously to sheer rock faces. Mount Orville rises 10,500 feet above sea level, part of the massive Fairweather Range, feeding Johns Hopkins Glacier. In this wilderness, the slow, grinding action of glaciers is alive and well; dark moraines snake down atop the glaciers, carrying pulverized pieces of mountain to the sea. Jagged ice pinnacles, or seracs, stretch into the sky like rows of killer whale teeth. The cascading ice speaks in creaks, groans, shot-like cracks, and thunderous booms, as blue-white walls of ice collapse into the sea in a process known as calving.

Vulnerable to falling ice in my small kayak, I remain a few miles away from the snouts of Gilman and Johns Hopkins Glaciers. I've been negotiating around icebergs for miles, and the ice pack is getting too thick to safely approach closer. A swell from the impact of ice falling from the terminus of Johns Hopkins Glacier lifts my boat ever so slightly. Even 3 miles away, the force of ice toppling into the sea resonates through its waters. It's amazing to think that this fjord was formed by an ice sheet that rose several thousand feet above and below me, carving deep into rock, even gouging the ocean floor. As the ice melted, seawater flooded the valley, creating a new waterway.

I feel an intimate part of this universe of ice, as seals grunt and cry out from atop nearby icebergs. All around, crystalline jewels pop, drip, split, roll over. Remembering that I can see only the tip of the iceberg—another 90 percent of it lies underwater—I stay well away from the bergy bits. In the distance, I see a large cruise ship approaching from the east end of the fjord. It is about to cover in less than an hour the distance I've just taken 5 hours to paddle. Despite its size, the ship seems dwarfed here; clearly, I am. Whether standing at the rail of a cruise ship or sitting in a 16-foot fiberglass sea kayak, it's easy to be humbled by the immensity of this place.

With its icy peaks, rivers of ice, massive headlands, precipitous valley walls, and shimmering bays flecked with ice, Glacier Bay encompasses a mythic landscape that takes you back to a time when ice ruled the continent. During the Wisconsin Ice Age, which ended about 10,000 years

ago, vast ice sheets covered much of northern North America and Europe and most of Southeast Alaska. As the climate warmed, the ice retreated and forests grew upon the land. About 3,500 years ago, the climate turned cold again. Snow accumulated in the coastal mountains, sending great glaciers across the land

▲ ICEBERGS ARE SCULPTED INTO BEAUTIFUL SHAPES BY WATER AND WEATHER.

once more. This neoglacial period, commonly called the Little Ice Age, sent a 20-mile-wide ice sheet all the way out into Icy Strait. By the late 18th century, the glacier lost its momentum in the strong currents and deep ocean basin and began a rapid retreat. The fjords formed at an astounding rate, reaching 65 miles into the mountains in just 200 years. Still a stronghold of the ice age, many of Glacier Bay's rivers of ice are melting back (retreating), while several are growing longer (advancing).

There are currently 13 active, calving tidewater glaciers (glaciers that terminate in the sea) within Glacier Bay proper and another 3 tidewater glaciers on the Gulf of Alaska coast. Of these, 6 are advancing, 7 are stable, and 3 are in retreat. In the southern inlets of Glacier Bay, many of the tidewater and valley glaciers (glaciers that flow down mountain valleys) have shrunk drastically.

Muir Glacier has been retreating for more than 200 years and appears to be in an advanced stage of deglaciation. Muir reached its maximum length of about 80 miles in the mid-18th century. When English explorer George Vancouver sailed through Icy Strait in 1794, it had already

text continues page 28

WHAT ARE GLACIERS AND HOW DO THEY MOVE?

Glaciers are slow-moving rivers of ice, born from snowfall in the mountains, that expand and contract, advance and recede, in reaction to the climate. They form where the air temperature stays cool enough to prevent annual snowfall from melting. At Glacier Bay, high precipitation and high peaks have created one of the world's densest mass of glaciers. Relentlessly, snowfall covers the mountains, compressing and metamorphosing into large glacier ice crystals. In Alaska, this process can occur within 30 to 50 years because of the high precipitation and temperate climate. By contrast, the process may take as long as 3,500 years in Antarctica because of aridity and extreme cold.

▼ A KAYAKER IS DWARFED BY GLACIALLY SCOURED CLIFFS IN JOHNS HOPKINS INLET.

How do glaciers travel? The sheer weight of the ice and the pull of gravity move glaciers gradually downward like conveyor belts: they

accumulate, transport, and dispose of ice and rock, scooping out U-shaped valleys from bedrock and leaving piles of debris in their wake. Imagine toothpaste squeezed from a tube: moving downhill, it bends and flows around objects in its path. Glaciers move by basal sliding and plastic flow. A glacier is actually sliding across the ground on a very thin film of water. Far below the surface, 100 to 200 feet down, highly pressurized ice is somewhat elastic. On the surface, however, ice is brittle, and when it pours down a steep slope or flows around a corner, it breaks. That's why you see crevasses and icefalls—the glacier is moving, fracturing as it travels down-valley.

The thicker the ice, the faster it moves. Glaciers tend to move faster in the center. Often you can see many crevasses along their sides, where slower-moving ice cannot keep up with medial movement. Glaciers generally move along the path of least resistance, although they have the power to ride up and over obstacles in their paths. As a glacier moves downhill along the sides of mountains, it picks up tons of broken rock. This rock debris, or moraine, is carried along on or frozen inside the glacier. It gives ice the power to erode the valley it travels through. At the bottom of a glacier there is a layer of ice laden with rock and debris. This glacier sole becomes an abrasive tool that scours, erodes, and cuts striations into bedrock. You'll see gouged lines from glacial scouring along the sides of rock faces in Glacier Bay's fjords. You can also see polished rock faces, worn smooth from sand and gravel constantly moving over them.

Once at tidewater, glaciers advance into the sea by pushing a protective moraine in front of the ice. A glacier "bulldozes" outwash material—rock, silt, and sand—and shoves it out; then it travels farther. The speed a glacier travels, whether advancing or retreating, depends on precipitation, the steepness of the valley through which it flows, and the depth of the water at its terminus.

melted back several miles. By 1890, it was only 40 miles long. In the past 100 years it has receded another 28 miles, and today, 4 large tributary glaciers are independent of Muir's main trunk. This is the greatest known recession of any valley glacier in the temperate regions of the world. In 1960, Muir and Riggs Glaciers were connected. Since then, Muir has retreated more than 7 miles, and it is about to leave tidewater.

Riggs Glacier, too, has shrunk, but has been near its present location since the late 1960s. Outwash streams have been building a delta in front of the terminus, and the glacier shows signs of advancing. Riggs flows 16 miles down a steep slope, and gravity seems capable of keeping the glacier's terminus in equilibrium. For years, we've watched dark bedrock slowly protrude from the face of Riggs. Each year, a little more rock reveals itself; you can climb right up the rock face and overlook blocky crevasses on the glacier.

Twenty years ago, **McBride Glacier** was a solid wall of ice extending into Muir Inlet. Today, a new fjord exists with a gravel spit extending out where the terminus used to be, and McBride continues to shrink. Wachusett Inlet, on the west side of Muir Inlet, was created by the rapid retreat of **Plateau Glacier.** Plateau retreated 12 miles in about 50 years; it finally stopped calving into tidewater in the mid-1970s and melted away.

▼ VISITORS WATCH ICE CALVING FROM MARGERIE GLACIER'S TERMINUS.

◆◆◆◆◆◆◆◆◆◆◆◆◆◆◆◆◆◆◆◆◆◆◆◆

WHY IS GLACIER ICE BLUE?

Glacier ice, so translucent, shimmers with deep blue hues because of the way light passes through it. Ice crystals absorb all colors of the spectrum, reflecting only the short blue wavelengths of light. So, we see blue ice. On overcast days, the color is especially intense. Icebergs that have been floating in the sea for any length of time begin to deteriorate; salt water and tidal movement cause the ice crystals to melt and become more porous. This ice—and any ice that contains air bubbles because it is rapidly losing its density—appears white rather than blue.

Today's maps show water where a glacier calved into the sea less than 25 years ago.

Two spectacular calving glaciers flow into Tarr Inlet. **Grand Pacific** and **Margerie Glaciers** were joined as one until about 1912, when Grand Pacific continued retreating. Within a few years it had retreated into Canada, where it remained until 1948, when it finally inched back over the border. Grand Pacific has the unique distinction of being the only tidewater glacier in Alaska that periodically crosses an international border. Today the two glaciers are joined again, after more than 80 years of separation. Margerie may begin to advance more rapidly now that it is joined with Grand Pacific. Margerie has a very conspicuous icefall. The steep gradient and constricted "channel" between mountain ridges break the glacier into a highly photogenic chaos of crevasses and seracs as it cascades down the mountain.

Johns Hopkins Inlet is the most spectacular visual ice feast in the bay. A series of high-altitude basins below a headwall of peaks extending from Mount Quincy Adams (13,560 feet) to Mount Crillon (12,726 feet) feeds the glaciers flowing into the inlet. Two centuries ago, ice filled the fjord to 6,000 feet above sea level, so that only the highest mountain peaks rose above the ice fields. Now the peaks seem to rise directly out of the sea. Ten glaciers cascade down from rocky heights in the short space of 10 miles, some of them actively calving into tidewater, beginning with **Lamplugh Glacier** at the mouth of Johns Hopkins. Rounding Confusion and Jaw Points, **Toyatte, Kadachan,** and **Tyeen** are visible to the northwest. On the southwest side of the fjord, **Kashoto, Hoonah,** and **Gilman** are all actively calving, and front and center is **Johns Hopkins. John** and **Clark** are small valley glaciers whose snouts lie high above tidewater. When Muir visited Glacier Bay, Johns Hopkins Inlet was one massive ice front. In 50 years, the ice retreated more than 11 miles; then, by 1935, it slowed its retreat. In the past 50 years, Hopkins has readvanced more than 2 miles. At the southernmost end of the inlet, in front of Gilman Glacier, the fjord is more than 1,200 feet deep, the result of glacial erosion from Johns Hopkins.

Reid Inlet, off the West Arm, is a couple of miles long and embraces 1 glacier. **Reid Glacier** deposited a large terminal moraine at the mouth of the inlet in the first 2 decades of the 20th century. Then, for the next 50 years, the ice front remained stationary. In 1980, Reid began a slow advance. Today it appears to be in equilibrium again, or advancing slightly.

GALLOPING GLACIERS

Sometimes glaciers surge suddenly, moving 10 to 100 times faster than their normal rate of flow, moving 100 or more feet per day. At least 10 glaciers in Glacier Bay have recently surged. Three have a fascinating repetitive pattern. Carroll and Rendu are valley glaciers in Queen and Rendu Inlets, respectively; Tyeen is a small hanging glacier in Johns Hopkins Inlet. During the past 50 years, all 3 have surged every 15 to 20 years. Carroll and Rendu push forward visibly or become noticeably more crevassed, while Tyeen pushes nearly a mile out of its valley, descending to tidewater. Each surge ends a year or so after it begins, and the glacier termini stagnate or shrink. Scientists believe surges are caused by meltwater trapped beneath the glacier, causing it to slide rapidly downhill.

Brady Glacier lies outside Glacier Bay proper, but is no less a dynamic part of its geology. Brady is the birthplace of Reid and Lamplugh Glaciers; its massive ice field covers 175 square miles and is fed by many of the Fairweather peaks. Its broad, relatively smooth plain has enticed skiers and mountaineers to penetrate its icy silence. In 1794, Brady was at tidewater, and it continued to advance into the sea throughout the 19th century, moving ahead by 4 miles. Brady continues to advance slowly. Incredible amounts of silt and sediment flow into Taylor Bay, making it a hazard for navigation. Waters near the terminus of the glacier are shallow and fraught with unpredictable currents from many braided outwash streams. Parts of Taylor Bay that were a few hundred feet deep 70 years ago are now covered by mudflats. These shallows prevent Brady from calving ice into tidewater; rather, ice melts off the terminus of the glacier.

Fifteen-mile-long **LaPerouse Glacier,** which flows off Mounts Dagelet and LaPerouse, is the only tidewater glacier in North America that calves directly into the open Pacific Ocean. It is named after French explorer Jean Francois de Galóup, Comte de La Pérouse, who explored along the outer coast and sailed into Lituya Bay in 1786, and who also produced the first detailed maps of Lituya Bay and wrote the first detailed descriptions of the Tlingit inhabitants. In 1966, LaPerouse Glacier surged to the low-tide line and its 250-foot-high face met the ocean surf

▲ MOUNT LAPEROUSE RISES ABOVE BRADY GLACIER.

head-on. Today, it fluctuates back and forth, usually within the tidal zone. At times, it is possible to walk in front of the $3\frac{1}{2}$-mile-wide face.

Lituya Bay, a dramatic T-shaped fjord on the outer coast, is the home of 2 tidewater glaciers. **North Crillon** and **Lituya Glaciers** are advancing over their outwash sediments.

Every year we see an entirely different Glacier Bay, amidst changes brought on by the centuries-long advance and retreat of ice. In some places the retreat is so recent that vegetation has hardly had a chance to gain a foothold. In other places, rain forest has returned to clothe the land.

Will a great ice age return again? Is our climate getting warmer? Some scientists insist the 20th century has been the warmest of the past 40 centuries, and they predict even warmer temperatures in the 21st century. Just as continued low temperatures during past ice ages brought the sea level down, revealing new land masses, so, too, could higher temperatures increase melting of the world's glaciers, flooding our coasts. No one knows for sure. It would take only a minor decrease in temperature and a minor increase in precipitation to trigger major growth of Alaska's glaciers. Meanwhile, Glacier Bay is continually being created, as the ancient ice age architects etch their grand designs upon the landscape.

▼ LITUYA GLACIER CONTINUES TO ADVANCE INTO LITUYA BAY.

GLACIER-SPEAK

ADVANCING GLACIER: Glacier that is moving down-slope, or pushing farther out into a fjord, as a result of snowfall feeding the glacier high in the mountains.

BERGY BIT: Rounded iceberg, the size of a small house, that floats with less than 15 feet showing above sea level.

CALVING: Process by which ice breaks off from the terminus of a glacier, usually into tidewater, rivers, or lakes.

CREVASSE: Deep, elongated crack in the surface of a glacier created by the stress of glacier movement.

FJORD: Deep arm of the sea filling a glaciated U-shaped coastal mountain valley.

GLACIAL REBOUND: Elastic, isostatic uplift of an area previously depressed by an ice sheet.

GLACIAL TILL: Unsorted, unstratified accumulations of sand, rock, and boulders deposited by melting glaciers.

GLACIER MILK: Extremely fine rock debris (silt) that gives a milky color to bodies of water fed by glaciers.

INTERGLACIAL FOREST: Forest that grew during a warmer period in an area once covered by glaciers and that subsequently was overrun by readvancing ice.

MORAINE: Rock debris transported by a glacier and dropped when the ice melts. A *lateral moraine* lies along the edge of a glacier; a *medial moraine* forms where the lateral moraines of 2 converging glaciers meet; a *terminal moraine* is the material deposited in front of a glacier.

OUTWASH: Glacial sediment (rock, silt, sand) sorted by size and deposited by glacial meltwater.

OUTWASH PLAIN: Broad, gently sloping plain.

RETREATING GLACIER: A glacier that is melting as a result of decreasing snowfall or higher temperatures, causing the glacier to melt faster than snow can accumulate high in the mountains. Also called *receding glacier.*

SERAC: Pinnacle of ice formed by the intersection of crevasses.

STRIATIONS: Scratches or grooves carved into rock that was scraped by glaciers.

TERMINUS: Glacier's lowest end. Also *snout.*

FLORA IN TRANSITION

Imagine going back to the end of the Wisconsin Ice Age, 10,000 years ago, when ice-covered landscapes were just emerging, the glaciers having left behind scraped bedrock and piles of gravel devoid of life. At the icebound heads of Glacier Bay's fjords, you can glimpse the processes that shape the earth. Like being in a reverse time machine, you can travel up Glacier Bay from Bartlett Cove to the uppermost glaciers and see the grand succession of life as plant communities reclaim the land. At Bartlett Cove, a 200-year-old forest houses Sitka spruce you can barely stretch your arms around, as well as hefty hemlocks 3 feet in diameter. Where a 300-foot-high river of ice stood just a moment ago in time, now stands a rich forest where birds sing and bears roam; yet 65 miles away, at the farthest reaches of Muir and Johns Hopkins Inlets, lie desolate landscapes where elemental rock stands naked.

On jumbled bare rock and in pools of water warmed by the sun, postglacial plant succession begins, as a black crust of felt-like algae clings to silt and rock, followed by light green lichens and yellow-green moss that have migrated in on the wind. Meanwhile, feathery, airborne seeds of yellow dryas, a remarkable pioneer, settle into moraines and outwashes. Dryas is the first plant to fully lay claim to the land. A prostrate perennial, dryas spreads into ever-expanding rosettes, eventually

◄ RAIN FOREST RECLAIMS LAND COVERED BY GLACIERS 250 YEARS AGO.

ALDER, HUMBLER OF HUMANS

Decades ago, the remarkable retreat of Muir Glacier created a vast moonscape that provided limitless opportunities for hiking. Today, much of that open terrain is covered with thick brush. Except where ice has recently retreated, leaving scoured rock, hiking upland off the beaches in Glacier Bay often involves intimate encounters with alder. There are incredible bodies of water, ice, and land to explore in both Muir Inlet and the West Arm; the problem is thick brush separates the beaches from many destinations. Dense alder thickets are practically impenetrable because their branches grow both horizontally and vertically. Often found growing next to, under, and up through the branches are spiny devil's club, salmonberry (also with sharp spines), and tall ferns.

Mountaineers seeking the high peaks of the Fairweather Range discover that one of the most difficult tasks on an expedition is the approach through miles of alder-choked brush growing atop glacial moraines. When making my way through alder thickets I sometimes wear thick rubber gloves and heavy, rubberized raingear—the kind worn by commercial fishers—when clawing through particularly voracious brush. Persistence has its rewards. A few miles of alder thrashing can take you into subalpine terrain. There, you'll discover lush meadows of colorful perennial wildflowers—false hellebore, shooting star, Sitka burnet, monkshood, fleabane, gentian, buttercup, and roseroot. Higher up, you'll find low-growing mats of heather, crowberry, and moss campion, as well as luetkea, saxifrage, and mountain harebell, and spectacular views of mountain peaks and glaciers.

forming a continuous blanket of vegetation. Matted roots stabilize outwash plains and glacial till and draw nitrogen from the air, releasing it into the soil, thus fortifying the soil for other plants to flourish. Dwarf fireweed and horse-tail nestle into gravel beds, and in no time, red soapberries add more color and variety to the blend of pioneering plants that foliate the landscape. Seeds of ryegrass move in on the tide, colonizing barren beaches. Birds and wildlife assist in spreading the seeds of succession, and within 3 to 4 decades, Sitka alder takes root, also drawing nitrogen from the atmosphere and eventually depositing it into the soil. Willows, too, establish themselves.

Within several decades, alders form dense, nearly impenetrable thickets, growing so tall and ropy that they cannot hold themselves upright any longer. Cottonwoods move in, cutting off sunlight to the alders and willows, their leaves adding to the growing layer of topsoil. As more nitrogen becomes available, slow-growing spruce and hemlock take hold, overpowering the other species. As the spruce begin towering over deciduous trees, falling spruce needles add acid to the layer of peat building at the base of the forest. Ironically, spruce cannot tolerate acidic soil, so they don't regenerate successfully. Western

▼ DRYAS STABILIZES BARREN LANDSCAPES AS GLACIERS RECEDE.

text continues page 40

FIREWEED

Spreading across tidal meadows, river-banks, gravel bars, and disturbed areas, fireweed finds a home in settings that many plants find inhospitable. No soil is too thin for this elegant magenta beauty, which gets its name from its ability to revegetate a burned-over landscape quickly after a fire. Two species grow in Glacier Bay country. Tall fireweed is found scattered across glacial barrens and in dense patches above beach meadows. Plants reach 6 feet in height with clusters of pink-purple flowers that last nearly all summer long, blooming from the bottom up. Dwarf fireweed, known as river beauty, livens recently deglaciated landscapes with its nearly fluorescent hue and blankets shorelines along fjords, rivers, and streams. Since fireweed is edible, I like to add their colorful flowers to my salads when I'm camping.

ROSEROOT

Roseroot is a succulent wildflower that grows on rocky cliffs and alpine areas all over Glacier Bay, as well as throughout Alaska, the Yukon, and the Pacific Northwest. With its light green, fleshy leaves spiraling in a rosette around a dark red crown of flowers, it looks more like a manicured houseplant than a hardy wildflower that is capable of rooting in even the tiniest cranny. Roseroot, which gets its name from its fragrant roots, is one of more than 600 species worldwide in the stonecrop family. If you're wandering in the backcountry, it's comforting to know that roseroot leaves are edible. Chopped raw in salads or cooked in a soup or stew, they'll add vitamins A and C to your diet. If you cut or burn yourself, you can squeeze a leaf or chew on a root and apply the soothing juice to your injury.

SUNDEW, THE CARNIVOROUS PLANT

You'll have to get down on all fours to find sundews! Flourishing in acidic bogs and wet meadows, the sundews (round-leaved and long-leaved) have tiny, white blossoms that appear in early summer and open only when the sun is shining. Their curved leaves have hundreds of spiky, red glands that secrete droplets of a thick, glue-like substance. Woe to the hapless insect that happens to land upon a sundew leaf; the spiked glands curl slowly inward around the insect as it struggles to free itself from the glue. The glands secrete digestive enzymes and soon the insect is history. Round-leaved sundews even catch spiders and crawling insects, simply by holding their leaves flat on the ground. Why would a plant capable of photosynthesis evolve to eat insects? Acidic muskeg areas are low in nitrogen and phosphorus; since insects are full of these nutrients, their ingestion allows sundews to live successfully in an acidic, nutrient-poor habitat.

INDIAN PAINTBRUSH

Indian paintbrush displays incredible color variation among the more than a dozen species growing in Alaska's coastal and alpine meadows and salt marshes. Around Gustavus and in the park and preserve, you can find paintbrushes ranging from light yellow to orange, and from light pink to crimson red. The colorful flower-like display

is actually the hairy bracts; the plants' small flowers are nestled inside the bracts. Paintbrushes are semiparasitic, living off the nitrogen produced by other plants. This may explain why paintbrushes often bloom among yellow dryas flowers.

hemlock rise above the spruce forest, and in their shade, the spruce succumb. In a rain forest more than 200 years old like the one in Bartlett Cove, spruce are slowly being replaced by shade-tolerant hemlock. Spruce topple, forming nurse logs for such forest shrubs as huckleberry, blueberry, salmonberry, devil's club, and more hemlock. Hemlock dominates the forest after about 600 years and may continue to grow for several hundred more years.

Muir Inlet and its tributaries are well into the alder thicket stage, with scattered cottonwoods and spruce gaining footholds. Open to the prevailing moist southerly winds, the inlet is a catchment basin for airborne seeds. In contrast, the West Arm is more insulated from ocean-borne winds, with the Fairweather Range acting as a barrier to moisture, sending down cold, dry winds from the heights. As a result, the West Arm still has a somewhat open appearance. Willow and soapberry bushes rise above a carpet of dryas, sphagnum moss, and bearberry. Open meadows of strawberries and flowering plants, like cow parsnip, lupine, and Indian paintbrush, draw bears and hikers alike. Alders and spruce are slowly creeping in.

Paludification, the creation of muskeg (peat bogs), is under way in parts of the Bartlett Cove forest as sphagnum mosses spread, accumulating moisture and cutting off oxygen to tree roots, causing hemlocks to die. Take a walk to Blackwater Pond on the forest trail from Bartlett Cove and you'll begin to understand the transition to muskeg. The pond was formed as rain and meltwater collected in a depression that once held a chunk of glacier ice. As the pond fills with organic material, drainage is impeded and the water level rises, thus drowning trees. Far from being a dead zone, the pond attracts waterfowl and songbirds. Today's forest, festooned in moss, has a spiritual silence to it, broken only by the chattering of a red squirrel or a raven's deep call. Shafts of sunlight penetrate to support tiny flowering plants such as twinflower, twisted stalk, coralroot, single delight, and lady's slipper.

The wonder of plant succession in Glacier Bay is that you can watch the world being created without human interference. Here, you can witness the processes that healed North America and Europe after ice age glaciers retreated more than 10,000 years ago.

INTERGLACIAL FORESTS

Before the Little Ice Age, a forest of spruce and hemlock covered much of the hills and valleys of Glacier Bay, similar to what you find throughout Southeast Alaska today. About 3,500 years ago, ice advanced down the valleys once again, sweeping the forest off mountainsides and burying lowland trees with glacial sediments and ice thousands of feet deep. For 3,000 years the forest lay buried. Then 2 centuries ago, when the glaciers began melting, their outwash streams cut through the deep deposits, exposing stands of ancient forests, many with bark and tiny branches still intact, with mosses clinging to them. The trees had been literally freeze-dried. As the glaciers continue to melt, more of these interglacial forests may reveal themselves. Their presence proves that Alaska's climate was appreciably milder in the past. Today, the cycle is about to come full circle, as alder, willow, and cottonwood take root around the decaying stumps and the land prepares a cradle for new spruce-hemlock forest.

◄ THE FOREST GROWS
AROUND A 3,000-
YEAR-OLD STUMP
THAT WAS REVEALED
WHEN THE GLACIERS
RETREATED.

WILDLIFE OF SHORE AND SKY

On a warm July afternoon, I walk the meadows above high tide in Bartlett Cove, heading south toward Point Gustavus. Ripe strawberries are the reason. Small, yet sweet as nectar, they bring me down on all fours to pick. Inching along among the low plants, I pause to pick and eat, pick and save. In time, there are 2 quarts in my plastic bowl. I pause for the reward, eating them handful by handful until they are gone. Satiated, I fall onto my back in the warm sun and into slumber. Later, I awake, sensing a presence in the light breeze wafting toward me. I rise up slowly, barely breathing, and there, just 15 feet from me, stands a black bear. Its cinnamon-tinted fur glistens in the sunlight. Adrenaline racing, I freeze, pondering what course of action to take, while the bear feeds on ryegrass, seemingly unmindful of my presence. Quietly, I snap a photo, then wait; the bear moves on, as silently as it arrived. Taking a deep breath, I retrieve my empty bowl and follow the shore back to Bartlett Cove.

From the tiny deer mouse to the imposing brown (grizzly) bear, Glacier Bay supports at least 28 mammal species. Here, wildlife is managed to maintain its natural state unmanipulated by humans, allowing successional changes, population fluctuations, mortality, and predator-prey relationships to exist. Hunting is not allowed, except in the Dry Bay Preserve. Glacier Bay is one of the few areas in

◄ A BROWN BEAR IN THE ALDER.

IS IT A BLACK BEAR
OR A BROWN BEAR?

Both black and brown (grizzly) bears range freely throughout the park and preserve, feeding on plants and animals. Brown bears, the largest omnivores in the world, are more commonly seen in the northern parts of the park and on the outer coast. Black bears are more common along the lower bay. Contrary to the old adage that black bears live only in the forest, I've seen them roaming the glacial barrens of upper Muir Inlet. In early summer, bears feed on roots and young shoots on snow-free, south-facing slopes; as the snow melts, brown bears search for succulent shoots at higher elevations, and black bears browse in the forest. By midsummer, both species seek out strawberry meadows. Constantly foraging the tide line in search of mussels and crabs, and feeding on horsetail and ryegrass, bears congregate along streams in late summer to gorge on migrating salmon.

Black bears are not always black, nor are brown bears always brown. Both range from blonde to cinnamon, brown, or black. Only a few people have ever caught a glimpse of a rare form of black bear with silvery blue fur. These "glacier bears" are found only on the narrow outer coastal forelands and up the Tatshenshini and Alsek River Valleys as far inland as British Columbia. The best way to differentiate between brown and black bears is by their profile. A brown bear has a hump behind its neck and a dish face or curved face; a black bear has a straight nose and no shoulder hump. Kayakers beware: bears swim in fresh or salt water and regularly move between the mainland and islands.

Southeast Alaska where wetlands are fully protected and forests will never be lost to clear-cut logging. Even trees infected with spruce bark beetle are left as is (this also enables scientists to study the role of the beetle in forest ecology).

It's exciting to witness the natural changes that occur

in wildlife populations as plant succession occurs. When I first explored Glacier Bay 24 years ago, brown bears and moose were extremely rare along Muir Inlet. As willows seeded themselves, growing into dense thickets, moose moved in to browse, with wolves, their prime predator, close on their heels. As plant succession continues up the bay and willow gives way to spruce and hemlock, moose populations may decline, and other bird and animal species will flourish in the evolving ecosystem. Wildlife is still dispersing throughout the park: over time, if the glaciers don't advance down the bay in the next couple of hundred years or so, Glacier Bay may look like more mature areas of Southeast Alaska.

While beaches are natural wildlife corridors and one of the easiest places to spot wildlife from a boat, you can find wildlife just about anywhere in the park. I've seen bears on glaciers and toads floating in the Tatshenshini River. On steep slopes above Tidal Inlet and on Mount Wright, mountain goats hop across stony ridges and moose forage among willows. Hoary marmots inhabit rocky slopes and alpine meadows, along with elusive wolverines, which favor the lush vegetation on mountainsides yet can also be found scavenging on beaches or hunting in the forest for grouse or snowshoe hare. Sitka black-tailed deer are recent newcomers to Glacier Bay, and

▼ THE PHOTOGRAPHER CATCHES A PORCUPINE NEAR THE ALSEK RIVER .

along with porcupines, martens, and red squirrels they inhabit the forested lands of lower Glacier Bay and from Point Carolus to the outer coast. In the Tatshenshini River and Alsek River corridors, Interior species have migrated downriver, and there you're more likely to see beavers, lynx, snowshoe hares, and red foxes. If you're cruising on Glacier Bay, keep a lookout for coyotes, wolves, red foxes, short-tailed and least weasels, minks, and river otters, which often comb the beaches for carrion, barnacles, sea urchins, and mussels.

One of Glacier Bay's smallest mammals, the wandering shrew, is the first to colonize recently deglaciated landscapes. Other tiny inhabitants you may see are the masked shrew and northern water shrew. Spend quiet time in the forest and you may observe northern red-backed voles, deer mice, and, in the evening, little brown bats. The boreal (western) toad is Glacier Bay's only amphibian. This warty creature lives on land, feeding on insects, yet is occasionally found swimming across formidable stretches of fresh or salt water.

ICEWORMS?

One day during the summer of 1887, Professor G. F. Wright of Oberlin College was walking across Muir Glacier when he discovered worms on the surface of the ice. He soon realized that, despite their desolate environment, these worms were actually living *in* the ice. Iceworms are slim, inch-long, segmented worms that resemble baby earthworms. They are usually dark brown or black and move with apparent ease along minute, invisible margins between glacial ice crystals. Surviving best at near-freezing temperatures, they avoid direct sunlight and high temperatures by burrowing down into the ice during the day. In the winter, they burrow down to avoid freezing to death. Look for them on overcast days or in the evenings, when you can sometimes find them by the hundreds, feeding atop patches of red algae and pollen grains on the ice.

MOUNTAIN GOATS

With their woolly, white, insulating hair, thick in summer and winter, mountain goats are at home among Glacier Bay's steep terrain and rivers of ice. They have specialized split hooves, with hard outer rims and rubbery soles, allowing them to spread their feet wide and grip onto rocky toeholds. Mountain goats seem to move effortlessly, yet cautiously, up and down near-perpendicular rock and ice faces. They are often confused with Dall sheep, also white, which are not found in Southeast Alaska. But the two animals are easy to distinguish: mountain goats have long, shaggy hair and beards, black horns, massive chests, and legs that appear to be wearing fur pantaloons. The elegant ceremonial Chilkat blanket, traditionally made by the Tlingit, is woven from mountain goat hair.

Mountain goats are grazers, picking their way across rocky hillsides to get to choice patches of vegetation away from predators such as wolves, bears, and even eagles, which have been observed trying to knock small kids off cliffs. Single kids are born in June and can stand immediately upon birth. In summer, mountain goats eat grasses, lichens, and herbs. In winter, they usually descend from the heights and subsist on hemlock, alder, and fern roots. Look for them on open craggy areas, especially in the West Arm, where goats often traverse cliffs just above sea level.

Glacier Bay's avian inhabitants are hard to miss. Drawn to the bay's rich marine feeding grounds and pristine forests, more than 220 species frequent the park. In the 20-hour days of summer, the photosynthetic cycle supercharges nutrient- and oxygen-rich waters of the North Pacific. Sunlight converts water and carbohydrates into food for phytoplankton. Tidal movement and the upwelling of nutrients (mainly nitrates, silicates, and phosphates) to the surface in the shallows and at the edges of tidewater glaciers encourage an explosion of marine life. Many birds arrive in late spring, just in time to partake of the oceanic feast.

Approaching the Marble Islands by boat as you travel up Glacier Bay, the first thing you notice is the restless energy: puffins furiously beat their tiny wings as they drop off cliff edges; gulls wheel above the islands, their calls a cacophony of high-pitched alarm, the birds in constant movement. Remote islands and steep cliffs provide essential nesting sites for pigeon guillemots, black-legged kittiwakes, glaucous-winged and herring gulls, black oyster-catchers, pelagic cormorants, puffins, and murres. Birds are most abundant from the beginning of May to mid-September. Seabird colonies hatch their young by late June and the nests are empty by the first of September.

Many bird species, such as Canada geese, loons, and scoters, are flightless during their molting period and thus vulnerable to disturbance. Staying clear of beaches where these birds gather, and navigating boats around flocks of floating birds and cliffs of nesting seabirds, will lessen disturbance. Vessels and kayaks alike are prohibited from approaching within 100 yards of nesting seabirds, except at the south half of South Marble Island, where you may approach to within 50 yards. Many islands are closed to human visitation because of the presence of seabird colonies and their sensitivity to human disturbance. Check with park rangers for closures.

Along coastal beaches thousands of shorebirds feed. Red-necked phalaropes raft together, in groups of 10 to 1,000, spinning in tidal currents, while hundreds of white-winged and surf scoters flock together throughout the bay. More than 15,000 red-necked phalaropes have been counted in late summer. These, along with the common murre, whose numbers have exceeded 15,000 during winter counts, are the park's most abundant species. Largest bird in the park is the bald eagle, seen perching regally in spruce trees or drifting across the sky with out-spread wings. More than 200 eagle nests have been located at Glacier Bay, with up to 100 occupied in a typical year.

Black-legged kittiwakes nest on sheer rock cliffs. From 3,000 to 4,000 birds inhabit the kittiwake colony near Margerie Glacier. The most southerly summer range for the Kittlitz's murrelet is at Glacier Bay, where about 20 percent of the world's population spends time. Kittlitz's murrelets gather near tidewater glaciers and glacial river

PUFFINS!

With their bright red-and-yellow bills, orange feet, and black bodies with white faces and breasts, horned puffins look like clowns in tuxedos. Tufted puffins have a bohemian look, with blonde feather tufts sweeping off their **▲ HORNED PUFFINS SUN THEM-SELVES ON A ROCK.** white faces, bright red-orange beaks, orange feet, and jet black bodies. Tufted and horned puffins, generally considered to be oceanic species, breed on islands in the park, including the Marble Islands and Cenotaph Island in Lituya Bay. For nesting, tufted puffins choose dirt burrows, while horned puffins choose rock crevices, both high on cliffs. Puffins seem comical, vigorously flapping their wings to keep their heavy bodies aloft while ascending from the sea; yet their hydrodynamic shape allows them to dive hundreds of feet underwater to catch fish, propelling themselves with their wings. Once the nesting season is over, puffins return to the open sea.

ARCTIC TERNS

The migration of the arctic tern is one of the great natural wonders of the world. Summering throughout Alaska, northern Canada, and the northern polar regions and wintering in Patagonia and the Antarctic, arctic terns experience more daylight than any other creature. Every year they fly a 25,000-mile round-trip, seeking out the pristine breeding habitat and food-rich marine environments of both poles of the earth. Small and graceful, terns arrive in Alaska in May, choose mates, and nest quickly. At Glacier Bay, nests are little more than a shallow depression on a gravel bar or outwash. With or without eggs in it, a nest is difficult to detect.

I guarantee, though, that if you wander near arctic terns' breeding grounds, you'll be screeched at and attacked. Accidentally venturing onto the wrong beach, I've experienced their high-pitched, rasping cries, while ducking to avoid their dive-bombing attacks. A female lays two brownish to greenish speckled eggs and, with the help of her mate, incubates them until they hatch out about 23 days later. After a good 3 weeks of hiding in the brush and a diet of fish, insects, and invertebrates caught by their parents, young terns are ready to fly. Migration south begins again in August. By December, the terns are back in the southern polar regions.

▼ ARCTIC TERNS RESTING AFTER THEIR EPIC FLIGHT.

outwashes. Marbled murrelets number more than 7,000 in summer. This small, brown-speckled seabird is a threatened species in the Lower 48 states under the U.S. Endangered Species Act, at risk from excessive logging of their nesting habitat, old-growth forests, and from entrapment in commercial fishing gill nets.

From mid-July through August, thousands of Vancouver Canada geese, surf scoters, white-winged scoters, harlequin ducks, and other waterfowl molt in secluded inlets. During migration, ducks, geese, and shorebirds concentrate in tidal areas to feed, while sandhill cranes rest and feed on open tidelands and marshes near Gustavus.

Serious birders are bound to find activity in these particular places: the beaches, forest, and meadows along Bartlett Cove, Bartlett River Estuary, the tidal flats, meadows, and forests of Gustavus, the Beardslee Islands, the Marble Islands, Lone Island, Russell Island, the cliffs south of Margerie Glacier, Adams Inlet, Hugh Miller Inlet, Dundas Bay, Point Carolus, Point Gustavus, and Sitakaday Narrows.

A plethora of insect life hatches out each spring at Glacier Bay. Stone flies, caddis flies, mayflies, and more familiar species such as mosquitoes, hatch and live in their larval or nymph stages in freshwater ponds and streams, even in meltwater running off glaciers. Insects provide an aerial feast for birds, bats, toads, and even mammals such as foxes and bears, but they are often a challenge for humans. Aboard a boat, you needn't worry about insects, but take a beach walk on a still day and you may find yourself being swarmed by no-see-ums, tiny gnats that harass humans and animals alike. Mosquitoes, deerflies, horseflies, and white socks feed on flower nectar and plant juices. But after mating, females vie for blood with a vengeance; they need it to stimulate egg production. Even in the mountains, insect life prevails. Mosquitoes hatch out in late May and June, tapering off by July. No-see-ums and white socks have their heyday in July and August and can be especially irritating to backcountry campers. Deerflies and horseflies usually peak in August. Carry repellent or a head net for your forays into the country, as well as no-see-um-proof netting for your tent.

WILDLIFE OF THE SEA

Look," announces a park naturalist on the tour boat. "Humpback off the port bow! Look for the breathing spout at about 10 o'clock." Heads pop up and a minor stampede of humans clamors to the observation deck. I hear a muffled blow and glimpse a dissipating vapor spout. Minutes pass; a hundred eyes focus on the water's surface. Suddenly, the dark sea erupts, and the mountainous bulk of a whale thrusts into the air. Then, with a thunderous crash of spray and foam, it disappears into the deep, as the crowd exclaims, "Wow!"

Whales are the largest mammals in Glacier Bay, and the endangered humpback is a sight to behold, especially when its body is rising out of the water. Rich fjord waters provide vital links in the oceanic food chain for humpback whales, as well as for the smallest of invertebrates. In the bay's nutrient- and oxygen-rich waters supercharged by summer's long daylight hours, phytoplankton populations bloom, providing fodder for bacteria, which are in turn eaten by zooplankton. Copepods feed on plankton and are in turn eaten by herring and other fish. Then whales, porpoises, seals, and sea lions gorge on fish.

◄ A HUMPBACK WHALE BREACHES, THROWING HIS BODY OUT OF THE WATER.

The floor of Glacier Bay is undergoing constant change as it transforms from barren, glacially scoured rock to a rich marine ecosystem with hundreds of species. Even raw streams settle in their courses, allowing algae and other life to take hold and fish to spawn. Now, many species common to Southeast Alaska inhabit park waters. The most visible fish in the park are the anadromous species, such as chinook, pink, coho, sockeye, and king salmon, Dolly Varden char, and cutthroat trout. These species, along with halibut, are highly sought by sportfishers. Shrimp and 3 species of crab—tanner, king, and Dungeness—inhabit the bay.

Some of the most diverse wildlife forms are found in the intertidal zone, the marine area uncovered by low tides. Here, withstanding twice-daily tidal variations of up to 25 feet, live many species common along North Pacific shores. Most rocky, protected beaches harbor such species as starfish, hermit crabs, blue mussels, limpets, barnacles, and periwinkles. Blue mussels are eaten by birds and mammals and form an important link in Glacier Bay's food chain. Occasionally, human foragers consider a meal of blue mussels or clams, but run the risk of PSP (paralytic shellfish poisoning), caused by

▼ A SUN-FLOWER STARFISH MOVES ACROSS THE SAND AT BARTLETT COVE.

toxins manufactured by microscopic algae (dinoflagellates) that accumulate in the digestive glands of bivalves.

Mud and sand flats and open, wave-beaten beaches lack protected areas for starfish and other creatures. Animals that burrow under the sand, such as razor, little-neck, and butter clams, thrive in these areas. Marine worms also do well, having adapted to the environment more than 550 million years ago. If you have an opportunity to walk the shorelines of different parts of Glacier Bay, you'll see differences in the abundance and variety of inter-tidal life forms. The farther up the bay you go, the fewer species you encounter: mainly barnacles, blue mussels, and other creatures that tolerate low-salinity seawater. In older, more mature areas such as Bartlett Cove and the Beardslee Islands, you find well-established kelp beds and tidal areas brimming with anemone, clams, cockles, whelks, chitons, starfish, sponges, snails, segmented worms, sea urchins, Dungeness crabs, and fish such as sculpin and blenny eels. An early-morning walk at low tide along the shores and dock pilings of Bartlett Cove will reveal dozens of species.

Minke whales are found in Glacier Bay and through-out Alaska's ice-free waters in the summer, though they are not as numerous as humpbacks. Smaller and sleeker than humpbacks, they average 27 feet in length and weigh 7 tons. Little is known about their population; there may be about 9,000 in the North Pacific. Although they are protected under the Marine Mammal Protection Act, sadly they are still heavily commercially harvested in the Southern Hemisphere. The smallest baleen whale in the North Pacific, they swim fast and rarely approach boats. Unlike humpbacks, minkes don't show their flukes while diving. What you may notice is a tall, curved, steel gray or black dorsal fin appearing simultaneously with a low, inconspicuous blow. Minkes can live more than 50 years.

With its striking color contrast of black body and white chin and its prominent dorsal fin, the killer whale, or orca, is hard to mistake. These highly social mammals are in the Odontoceti family of toothed whales. The killer whale is actually the largest member of the dolphin family. Males grow much larger than females, reaching 25 feet in length and weighing up to 6 tons. You can tell a male from

text continues page 58

HUMPBACK WHALES

Humpbacks are migratory whales that live in all the world's oceans. They are members of the family Mysticeti, or baleen whales, and they are subgrouped as rorquals—large-volume feeders with no teeth—which include blue, fin, sei, and minke whales. To consume the prodigious amounts of food they require, numerous throat grooves expand as they open their mouths as much as 90 degrees, gulping up to 150 gallons of water at once and retaining the food while straining out the water through paired, comb-like baleen plates.

Humpbacks travel from winter calving grounds in Hawaii and Baja California to their favorite feeding spots in Southeast Alaska, where they spend 4 to 7 months gorging primarily on krill, shrimp, and schools of fish: herring, capelin, walleye pollock, and sand lance. Humpbacks don't feed year-round, so they must store enough fat in summer to last the rest of the year. They weigh 35 tons and stretch 50 feet in length, but their size hasn't prevented them from earning their reputation as the most acrobatic of whales. They roll on the surface, lobtail ("stand" on their heads and thrash the water with their flukes), spyhop (lift their heads vertically out of the water), and breach (leap into the air) more than any other species.

Humpbacks also utilize a unique feeding technique known as bubble-netting. One or more whales dive under a school of fish and swim in a circle, casting a net of bubbles from their blowholes around the fish. The bubbles confuse the prey briefly—long enough for the whales to lunge up through the bubble net, swallowing the collected fish.

Humpbacks, which may live 50 years, once numbered more than 15,000 in the North Pacific. Commercial hunting reduced their numbers to about 850 by the 1960s. In

1966, a worldwide moratorium on humpback whale hunting went into effect. By this time, the world's humpback population had dwindled from 125,000 animals to less than 10,000. The U.S. Endangered Species Act gave humpbacks federal protection in 1973, and since then, their numbers have steadily grown; still, there are only an estimated 1,200 in the North Pacific population. Humpbacks have been seen in Glacier Bay since at least the 1930s, and today, 15 to 35 feed seasonally in bay waters. Predictably, humpback whale numbers increase in Glacier Bay in mid-June and decrease in August. They have favorite annual feeding spots, such as Point Carolus, Bartlett Cove, the Beardslee Islands, Sitakaday Narrows, and Whidbey Passage.

Scientists are studying humpbacks in Glacier Bay and elsewhere in Southeast Alaska to determine to what extent an increase in boat traffic is negatively impacting them. As cruise ship size and numbers have increased dramatically in the bay over the years, the population of whales that summer in the bay varies, raising concerns about their well-being. Sound has an important function in communication among these most vocal of whales. In deep, constricted fjord waters, sound reverberates off submarine canyon walls. Is underwater noise created by cruise ships and other vessels driving these keenly sound-sensitive whales out of the bay? It is difficult to say whether short-term disturbances translate into abandonment of Glacier Bay as a feeding area or reduced survival and reproductive success.

Regardless of the answer, humpbacks—and all whales—deserve the highest protection, both in and outside park waters. The Park Service has established regulations governing the bay's "whale waters" in the lower bay. From May 15 to August 31 boats longer than 18 feet must maintain a midchannel course. When whale numbers in the bay increase, all boats must maintain a speed of 10 knots or less. Boats may not pursue whales and may not approach closer than a quarter mile to any whale.

a female by the male's taller, straighter dorsal fin; the female's is shorter and slightly curved back. The youngsters have the smaller dorsal fins. Killer whales travel in groups of up to 40 animals, called pods.

Glacier Bay has both resident and transient killer whale pods. Resident pods maintain definite home ranges, feeding primarily on fish, while transient pods travel widely, feeding more aggressively on marine mammals and molting seabirds. A pod cooperates in hunting and feeding efforts, using sharp teeth to corral and catch their prey. Just outside Glacier Bay, 4 killer whales attacked 2 moose swimming in Icy Strait. One was consumed, and the smaller moose escaped to a nearby kelp bed, only to drown later. Harbor seals and fish are the most abundant and dependable food source for killer whales in Glacier Bay, while sea otters, with their dense fur, lack of body fat, and musky odor, are rarely preyed upon.

In Glacier Bay–Icy Strait waters in recent years, 132 individual killer whales have been identified, representing 15 different pods. Two resident pods, with a combined total of 54 whales, have been regularly sighted. While you may not see them leaping over stone walls and doing back flips in front of your boat, as in the movie *Free Willy*, you may observe their acrobatic nature, as they commonly breach, spyhop, and lobtail, much like their distant cousins the humpbacks.

While Dall porpoises are rare in Glacier Bay, harbor porpoise concentrations are among the highest in Southeast Alaska, with estimated densities of 1 to 4 porpoises per square mile at times during the summer. If you notice porpoises bow-riding alongside your boat, they are likely stocky Dall porpoises; they can swim up to 30 miles per hour. People often mistake these porpoises for killer whales, since their coloration is similar. A Dall porpoise is much smaller than a killer whale, averaging 6 feet in length and 300 pounds, with smaller, triangular dorsal fins. The diminutive harbor porpoise, averaging 5 feet long and 120 pounds, is shy and avoids moving vessels; it generally travels alone or in small groups of a few porpoises. When conditions are quiet, you can hear harbor porpoises exhale between dives.

Sea lions and seals inhabit park waters and haul out on

◄ STELLER
SEA LIONS
GATHER IN
A RAUCOUS
HAREM,
DEFENDED
BY A
SINGLE
BULL.

prominent rock headlands and islands, allowing tour boats to observe them from a nonthreatening distance. Spotted harbor seals also haul out on icebergs. The Steller sea lion is a raucous, robust pinniped known for its gregarious behavior. An adult male can grow into a 1-ton mountain of flesh, despite the fact that he may fast for 2 months during the summer breeding season, when he mates with and defends his harem and territory from other males. Females give birth to a single pup between mid-May and July. Named for George Steller, the first to document the species in 1741, Steller sea lions' numbers have plummeted in recent decades, their population declining by 77 percent in Alaska in the past 30 years. In 1990, they were designated a threatened species under the U.S. Endangered

JOHNS HOPKINS INLET: HARBOR SEAL REFUGE

Glacier Bay has one of the largest known harbor seal breeding concentrations anywhere in Alaska, with a population estimate of 5,000 to 7,000. Harbor seals are the most numerous marine mammal in the bay; you'll see them hauled out on ice, sandbars, rocks, and reefs to rest, escape predators, breed, and pup (give birth). Averaging 6 feet in length and weighing 200 pounds, these seals exhibit variable color patterns, ranging from nearly white to nearly black with contrasting spots. They eat squid, shrimp, octopus, and schooling fish, as well as salmon. You can distinguish a seal from a sea lion. Sea lions have external ear flaps and jointed front and hind flippers that allow them to move with a clumsy sort of walk. And sea lions have noticeable whiskers and make a loud growly noise, which early explorers thought made them seem like lions.

Most seals, on the other hand, do not have visible external ears. They move on their short front flippers and back flippers by humping themselves forward like overweight caterpillars.

Pupping takes place on ice and at a few land haul-outs from late April through mid-June. Newborns can swim almost immediately after birth. Disturbance of the bond between mother and pup in the first week or so after birth can lead to permanent abandonment of the pup and consequent starvation. For this reason, Johns Hopkins Inlet is closed beyond Jaw Point to all boats from May 1 to June 30 and to cruise ships from July 1 to August 31. Seals are vulnerable to disturbance anytime and are easily spooked. A half-mile radius around the Spider Islands, part of the Beardslee Islands, is off-limits to humans. At all times, boats must maintain a distance of 0.25 nautical mile (570 yards) from seals hauled out on the ice.

Species Act. It would be optimistic, however, to say that Glacier Bay's sea lions are fully protected; like most marine mammals, they migrate throughout the North Pacific and so are vulnerable to competition with commercial fishing activities and entanglement in fishing nets. The best haul-out in the bay where you can observe sea lions is on the north side of South Marble Island. Elsewhere in the park, hundreds of sea lions and seals haul out on Graves Rocks, at Lituya Bay, and at Cape Fairweather.

Sea otters have recently found a home at the mouth of Glacier Bay. Formerly, tens of thousands of sea otters populated Southeast Alaska, but they were hunted to near-extinction from the mid-1700s to 1910 for their luxurious brown to black fur coats. In the 1970s, sea otters were reintroduced into the park, in Dicks Arm at Cape Spencer. Their numbers are increasing along Icy Strait, at the mouth of Glacier Bay, and among kelp beds on the outer coast and they continue to inhabit new territory. Otters generally feed in shallow water less than 100 feet deep. On the surface, these buoyant 5-foot-long, 70-pound balls of fur float on their back and carry their young on their belly. Look carefully and you might see an otter with an urchin in its paws, cracking it open on a rock atop its belly.

▼ A SEA OTTER RESTS IN A KELP BED TO HAVE ITS LUNCH.

TLINGIT HOMELAND

The Tlingit, traditionally occupying Southeast Alaska's island archipelago and mainland from the Stikine River to Icy Bay, are one of dozens of distinct Native peoples living on the temperate, forested Northwest Coast of North America. The Tlingit share many characteristics with other Pacific Northwest Coast peoples: linguistic similarities; a reliance on marine and coastal fish, mammals, shellfish, and plants; and highly developed woodworking, basketry, and weaving techniques. Three main Tlingit clans have occupied the region encompassing Glacier Bay: the Chookaneidí, Wooshkeetan, and T´akdeintaan.

Long ago, during the Little Ice Age or earlier, the Tlingit say, *S' é Shuyee*, the Edge of the Glacial Mud (what is now Glacier Bay), was a postglacial valley with grass growing in it. Near the mouth of the bay lay *Gathéeni*, Red Salmon River (where present-day Bartlett River lies). The people lived at *L'awshaa Shakee Aan*, Town on Top of the Glacial Sand Dunes (Bartlett Cove), and at *Chookanhéeni*, Straw Grass River (now Berg Bay). The clans lived in harmony with nature in a river valley abundant with salmon, whose source was a great glacier at the head of the valley.

◄ TLINGIT CHILDREN WITH DUGOUT CANOES EARLY IN THE 20TH CENTURY.

In one version of Glacier Bay history, a young girl, Kaasteen, lived in the village. When she reached puberty, she went into seclusion, in a traditional rite of passage. Out of loneliness she violated a taboo by calling the glacier's spirit far up the valley, unaware of the consequences. The ice fields began to move and advanced down the valley. Ice slapped against the clan houses, crushing them and toppling the forest with icebergs. The people held a council and decided to abandon their village before the unstoppable glacier reached it. They knew, however, that it would follow the one who called it. Kaasteen agreed to stay behind. Her relatives brought her food and clothing, and her grandmother, Shawatseek, offered to take Kaasteen's place, but Kaasteen refused. She acted with courage, staying behind to sacrifice herself for her people, thus redeeming herself and her people.

While the people sat in their canoes watching ice destroy the last houses, Kaasteen's house slid downward to the bottom of the ocean before their eyes. The glacier moved over her and she became one with its spirit, so that the rest of the people might live on. The clans settled at Excursion Inlet, Ground Hog Bay, and on North Chichagof Island, at a place they named *Hoonah*, which means In the Lee of the North Wind. To the Tlingit, Glacier Bay is sacred because it was purchased with the blood and spirit of Kaasteen, The Woman in the Ice. The spirit of all the Hoonah Tlingit remains there. The Tlingit say that when bergs fall into the bay you can sometimes see something bright in the water. These, it is said, are Kaasteen's ice children. With the retreat of the ice, the people renamed the bay *Sit´ ee ti Geiyí*, the Bay in Place of the Glacier. And so it passed that the Ice Age drove the people from their ancestral lands thousands of years ago.

Tlingit oral history attests to the presence of Native settlements inside what we now call Glacier Bay, though glaciers destroyed all evidence. Just outside the park boundary near Point Couverden lies a prehistoric site extending back 9,000 years. Ancestors of contemporary Hoonah Tlingit harvested seasonally bountiful resources in Glacier Bay and the surrounding region. The people had a detailed knowledge of geography, of animal behavior and life cycles, and of plants and their uses, and moved from camp to camp in a seasonal round of harvesting. Abundant and varied species provided them with a rich diet, including fish, mammals, birds, eggs, berries, and plants. When the tide went out, the "table was set": seaweed and shellfish could be picked up on the beach. Forests provided the raw materials for clothing, shelter, fuel, carved totems, tools, and utensils.

A rich natural environment allowed for leisure time, so highly refined art forms and an elaborate material culture developed. Tlingit tales of creation and history are tuned to ancient rhythms of wildlife and landscape. Humans, plants, animals, and landforms are embodied with the presence of mythological spirits. The existence of the land and its resources, and humankind's access to them, depends on the benevolence of these spirits. When the spirits are respected, the life forms in which they are embodied continue to return to the people. Today's Hoonah Tlingit honor and cherish this heritage, incorporating it into their daily lives.

Vigorous trade existed among Tlingit, Eyak, and Athabascan groups. The Tlingit traveled along the coast in huge dugout cedar canoes as long as 60 feet and able to carry up to 50 people. Since cedar did not grow this far north, they traded for canoes with the Tlingit living farther south near Ketchikan or with the Haida of the Queen Charlotte Islands. Seals, Steller sea lions, and sea otters were hunted for food and for their hides. The land (river) otter was never hunted or used for fur because the Tlingit believed

▼ TLINGIT SEALING CAMP AT BERG BAY, 1899.

◆◆◆◆◆◆◆◆◆◆◆◆◆◆◆◆◆◆◆◆◆◆

SPIRIT BEINGS

Kah H'lit-tu-yúh, the Man of Lituya, was a spirit being who dwelled in deep ocean caverns near the entrance to Lituya Bay. He resented any interlopers on the bay and would capture them, turning them into bears and making them his slaves. From the lofty heights of the Fairweather Mountains, these bears kept watch for approaching canoes, and together with *Kah H'lit-tu-yúh* they would grasp the water at the entrance to the bay and shake it as if it were a sheet, causing huge tidal waves to destroy the intruders. Sound like earthquakes and tidal waves? Anyone who travels to Lituya Bay by boat can appreciate *Kah H'lit-tu-yúh*'s turbulent currents, riptides, and evidence of seismic activity.

that lost or drowned people were turned into *Koostaa-kaa*, Land Otter Men. The Tlingit and Eyak traded seal and fish oil, otter pelts, bird beaks, and halibut to the Athabascans for copper, porcupine quills, red iron ochre, caribou hides, and animal furs. Northern Tlingit traded with the Southern Tlingit and Haida for carved cedar canoes, chests, food boxes, and dishes.

The Tlingit have hundreds of descriptive names for places in the park, but only a few names exist on today's maps. Only two, in fact, come directly from their language: Lituya Bay (from *H'lit-tu-yúh*, the Lake Within the Point, and Sitt-ghae Peak and Sitakaday Narrows (misspelled attempts at *Sit´ ee ti Geiyí*). Several peaks and glaciers are named after Tlingit guides and leaders: Tlingit Peak, Hoonah Glacier, Kashoto Glacier (after a chief of the Hoonahs, visited by John Muir in 1879), Toyatte Glacier (after the Stickeen nobleman and captain of Muir's Native guides to Glacier Bay in 1879), Tyeen Glacier (after the captain of Native guides on Muir's second trip to Glacier Bay in 1890), and Mount Kloh-Kutz (after the Chilkat Tlingit leader).

By the 1880s, just 140 years after the arrival of the first European explorers, the process of acculturation had altered Tlingit lifeways, and their pattern of seasonal movement changed. People settled into permanent villages. Adoption of European-style clothing reduced the need for animal hides, and commercial salmon canneries commandeered aboriginal fishing streams and hired Native workers. Guns, store-bought food, tools, utensils, conversion to Christianity, and the creation of schools changed life dramatically. While Americans discovered the wonders of Glacier Bay by steamboat, the Tlingit found themselves reduced to a curiosity in their ancestral hunting grounds or became caught up in the feverish fur trade. Seal-hunting camps became a tourist attraction, as steamship passengers found their tents, with seal skins on drying racks, photogenic. Along the outer coast, the Tlingit continued to hunt sea otters seasonally and sell their hides, until the animals (from Alaska to California) were virtually exterminated at the turn of the century.

Tlingit claims to ancestral fishing and hunting rights were eventually extinguished through a compensatory federal settlement after the bay became a national monument in 1925, though a few Natives continued to keep cabins, smokehouses, and scattered traplines in the bay, negotiating with the government for special privileges to continue seal hunting and gull egg gathering. The Marine Mammal Protection Act of 1972 once and for all prohibited the commercial harvest of seals, otters, or any marine mammals.

Today, a philosophical gap exists between the Park Service's preservation ethic and the Tlingit community's cultural identity with the landscape. One thinks in terms of wilderness preservation; the other views the landscape as a source of sustenance. To the Hoonah Tlingit, subsistence use of Glacier Bay is intimately tied to their cultural preservation. After years of alienation, the Park Service and the Hoonah are reconnecting. In 1987, George Dalton, a village elder, supervised the carving of a traditional spruce canoe in the park to commemorate Glacier Bay's earliest people. Dalton died in 1990, but his legacy lives on. Other elders have shared Tlingit culture with the Park Service. In 1995, the Hoonah Indian Association and the park signed a "memorandum of understanding," formally recognizing their commitment to explore avenues for managing our shared heritage.

7964

JOHN MUIR'S LEGACY

SIGHTSEEING, SCIENCE, AND CONSERVATION

Making notes and sketching in the fjord that would later bear his name, California naturalist John Muir wrote on a cold, stormy October day in 1879, "Sunshine streamed through the luminous fringes of the clouds and fell on the green waters of the fjord, the glittering bergs, the crystal bluffs of the two vast glaciers, the intensely white, far-spreading fields of ice, and the ineffable chaste and spiritual heights of the Fairweather Range, which were now hidden, now partly revealed, the whole making a picture of icy wildness unspeakably pure and sublime." His evocative prose, first published in the San Francisco *Evening Bulletin*, simultaneously spawned a flurry of sightseeing and of science and conservation interests in Glacier Bay that have continued for more than a century. While Muir was not the first non-Native traveler to Glacier Bay, he began a passionate love affair with it and popularized it through his writings in a way that would forever identify him with that grand landcape.

The son of a Scottish farmer, Muir studied for 3 years at the University of Wisconsin, discovering the new glacial theory of Louis Agassiz, a Swiss geologist teaching at Harvard who surmised that a single ice sheet had once covered much of the earth. Muir dropped out before graduating and traveled to California to wander among the mountains and moraines of the Sierra Nevada,

◄ EARLY GLACIER BAY VISITORS POSE BY MUIR GLACIER.

◀ JOHN
MUIR AND
SCIENTISTS AT
HIS CABIN
NEAR MUIR
POINT, 1890.

eventually writing a book inspired by Agassiz's work. He became convinced that Yosemite Valley had been created by glaciers. His ideas, however, were ridiculed by the scientific community. Poet, visionary, and self-made scientist, Muir set his sights to the north. With an adventurous spirit and an unquenchable thirst for scientific discovery, he set out to prove Agassiz's theory. His first trip was also somewhat of a pilgrimage; he wanted to immerse himself in wild country for the enlightenment it might bring him. He believed that living in and studying nature would transform people spiritually. Later writings would elaborate on his philosophy, which he referred to as his "glacial gospel." In Alaska, Muir came to understand deeply the connection between the earth and all its inhabitants—whatever we do to nature, we do to ourselves.

Muir was one of Alaska's first steamship visitors; not surprisingly, he found this mode of travel confining, referring to "the narrow bondage of a ship's deck" as a far cry from the freedom of wandering afoot in the Sierra Nevada. Still, he benefited from the modern conveyance of the day, mail steamer travel being the high-tech travel mode in 1879. Aboard ship, he longed for more intimate contact with the earth, sea, and sky.

Stepping off the ship in Fort Wrangell, Muir traveled in a 35-foot cedar dugout canoe to Hoonah with Presbyterian minister S. Hall Young, their guide Sitka

Charley, and three Tlingit paddlers. There, they heard stories from the Natives about rivers of ice and a bay filled with "white thunder." Muir urged the party on in the face of near-constant rain to *Sit´ ee ti G̱eiyí*. They encountered Hoonah Tlingit hunters laying in their winter store of seal meat and skins in Berg Bay, on the west shore of Glacier Bay.

Paddling farther into the mountain-rimmed bay that would soon be called Glacier Bay, they went on until the ice was too thick to continue. Muir leapt ashore and, in the waning days of October, came face to face with glaciers in ways that would amaze and transform him. In *Alaska Days with John Muir*, S. Hall Young wrote, "Muir would explore all day long, often rising hours before daylight and disappearing among the mountains, not coming to camp until after night had fallen. Again and again the Indians said that he was lost; but I had no fears for him. When he would return to camp he was so full of his discoveries and of the new facts garnered that he would talk until long into the night, almost forgetting to eat."

Muir returned to California, where his stories of adventure and discovery were serialized in the San Francisco newspaper. Muir invited Americans to discover the Alaskan wilderness. "Go," he wrote, "go and see." The public responded. In 1883, two years after Muir's second visit to Glacier Bay, Captain James Carroll brought the steamer *Idaho* on the first cruise to Glacier Bay, where sightseers marveled at the glaciers, fjords, mountains, plants, and wildlife to be found there. The 300-foot-high, 3-mile-wide glacier, now named Muir (as is the inlet), became the most renowned glacier in North America. With each boatload, more was written about the wonders of the Inside Passage.

In less than 20 years, Alaska had captured the imagination of the American public. By the turn of the century, steamships had carried more than 25,000 tourists to Glacier Bay. The trip became so popular that Captain Carroll had wooden walkways built along the terminal moraine of Muir Glacier for the tourists to venture onto the ice. But, suddenly, in September 1899, a huge earthquake rocked the Gulf of Alaska coast, and shock waves sent the Muir ice front into chaos. Calving was so heavy that ships could not approach the face of the glacier for many years. A few steamers tried to enter Glacier Bay in 1909, but ice conditions had changed drastically, making it difficult to approach, so they headed instead to Taku Glacier, south of Juneau.

THE WONDROUS SCENE: EARLY TOURISM

In the tradition of many a Victorian traveler of the day, writer Eliza Scidmore found her 1884 steamer trip up Alaska's Inside Passage to be exciting and educational. Writing one of the first travel guides to Alaska, she entertained readers with lavish descriptions. Of Muir Glacier, she wrote: "The vast, desolate stretch of gray ice visible across the top of the serrated wall of ice that faced us had a strange fascination, and the crack of the rending ice, the crash of the falling fragments, and a steady undertone like the boom of the great Yosemite Falls, added to the inspiration and excitement. . . . The great buttresses of ice that rose first from the water and touched the moraine were as solidly white as marble, veined and streaked with rocks and mud, but further on, as the pressure was greater, the color slowly deepened to turquoise and sapphire blues. The crashes of falling ice were magnificent at that point, and in a keen wind that blew over the icefield we sat on the rocks and watched the wondrous scene."

▼ SS QUEEN AT MUIR GLACER, c. 1896.

Tours to Glacier Bay did not resume again until the 1950s, when small boats carried passengers far up into Muir Inlet to see the then greatly reduced but still dramatically active Muir Glacier. Sightseeing in Glacier Bay National Park throughout the 1950s and 1960s, though, was minimal. In the early 1970s, cruise ship companies originating in Seattle and Vancouver toured the bay and its popularity grew astronomically. Until the mid-1970s, Muir Inlet was the main scenic attraction, but with the continued rapid retreat of Muir Glacier, the larger ships headed into the West Arm. By 1979 there were 100,000 visitors annually, and today, more than 300,000 people visit the park every year.

Just as the pioneering cruises to Glacier Bay laid the foundation for a visitor tradition in the park, so did the early naturalist expeditions establish a tradition of scientific discovery. Steamships carried the first scientists studying glacial geology, beginning in earnest with G. F. Wright's monthlong study at Muir Glacier in 1886 and culminating in the most famous scientific expedition of the century, the privately financed Harriman Alaska Expedition of 1899, which spent 2 months exploring the Alaska coast, including 5 days at Glacier Bay. John Muir, by then considered the world's greatest authority on glacial action, was one of 30 scientists, artists, and photographers—men such as paleontologist William H. Dall, ethnologist George B. Grinnell, geologist G. K. Gilbert, and photographer Edward S. Curtis—whose observations along the Alaska coast resulted in an 11-volume narrative of groundbreaking scientific observations in every field. Today's scientists continue in their footsteps.

Finally, while John Muir's early descriptions of sun-spangled, berg-filled fjord waters and unearthly mountains' splendor inspired sightseer and scientist alike, his most important legacy was his passionate zeal for wilderness and the natural world. As one of the fathers of the conservation movement, his vision spread not only to all who had the good fortune to know him, but also to generations hence, who were to read his timeless essays promoting personal stewardship of the earth.

THE OUTER COAST

The very mention of Glacier Bay National Park and Preserve's outer coast conjures up images of earthquakes, rough seas, boulder-strewn beaches, and tragic drownings in tide rips. Wild and desolate, the outer coast is one of the roughest and most exposed coastal areas in North America. Upon leaving the shelter of Cross Sound, running through the riptides of Inian Pass, and maneuvering around Cape Spencer, a boat of any size feels vulnerable.

Today we're on our first backcountry patrol of the season to the park's fabled outer coast. Evan Toscano-Jones and I are park rangers for territory covering a couple of hundred miles of coastline, from Point Carolus at the mouth of Glacier Bay to the Doame River, the southern boundary of Glacier Bay National Preserve. It's the first day of June, and the coast is windswept and rain-drenched. The temperature has reached a high 45°F, and southeast winds are blowing at 30 knots with a gale warning in effect for the Gulf of Alaska. We're with our supervisor, Dave Nemeth, running the Gulf of Alaska in one of the park's patrol vessels, *Drumlin*, a 31-foot cabined fiberglass motorboat.

◄ STORMY WEATHER HITS THIS STRIP OF COAST AT GLACIER BAY NATIONAL PARK.

There are few protected anchorages between the southern and northern park and preserve boundaries. While Graves Harbor, Torch Bay, and Dixon

Harbor are obvious indentations in the coast, they provide no safe anchorage during storms; Lituya Bay offers the only true safe harbor from the open ocean. Today's seas are the roughest I've ever maneuvered a boat in. With driving rain battering the windshield and seas rolling and breaking far offshore from rocky headlands, we move slowly up the coast, rocking, surfing, and pitching. Dave, Evan, and I trade hands at the wheel at regular intervals; I find it less intense when I'm steering because I remain totally focused on the present moment and haven't time to be seasick. Each wave presents itself and I steer up, over, and down it. A sooty shearwater flies along, skimming over the swells— the only living thing visible in the storm besides us.

By late afternoon we're near the entrance to Lituya Bay at La Chaussee Spit, known as "the Chopper." This long, narrow tongue of rock and gravel reaches across the shallow, treacherous entrance channel, nearly meeting Harbor Point, the opposite shore. Two orange markers show boats the way to enter the narrow passage without going aground, but there's no guarantee. Lituya Bay can be safely entered only during slack tide, for a half hour every 6 hours. At any other time, rip currents, like white water on a river, move across rocky shoals, running into heavy ocean swells as the 85-fathom-deep fjord empties or fills. Incoming surf meeting outgoing tide creates opportunities for disaster. At least 100 lives and many boats have been lost at the mouth of the bay. Fortunately, we've timed our arrival to coincide with slack tide. With Dave at the helm, we line up the boat with the markers and angle our way slowly into the bay, anchoring in the lee of Cenotaph Island.

The following day, the storm has cleared and we hike up a small stream east of La Chaussee Spit, identifying plants and looking for signs of moose and bear. Returning to the mouth of the stream, Evan and I encounter a brown bear. We're 30 feet away, raising our arms and talking to him, watching him rear up on his hind legs for a moment and then start walking toward us. Outwardly, I remain calm. What choice have I? Satisfied that we pose no threat, the brownie veers off into the brush.

After 6 days, we've seen 9 brownies—just a reminder of who this place really belongs to. We hike south along

GEOLOGY OF LITUYA BAY

Located halfway up the park's outer coast, Lituya Bay is 8 miles long, a deep submarine basin carved out eons ago by a great glacier. At its head lies a near-perpendicular 12,000-foot-high wall of ice and rock. At the base of the granite headwall, the bay splits into a T shape, with Lituya Glacier calving into the bay on the west, North Crillon Glacier on the east, and Cascade tumbling down from the center. The Fairweather and Queen Charlotte Faults meet deep under the T-shaped bay and slice through the Fairweather Range, creating an active seismic fracture zone where at least 5 massive slides of rock and ice have resulted from earthquakes and tsunamis in the past 150 years. The most recent earthquake, a 7.9 in 1958, created the largest tidal wave ever known to hit shore. A wall of water swept through the bay, splintering spruce and hemlock trees and stripping the shores of the bay to bedrock 1,720 feet up the mountainside. This single earthquake produced a 23-foot horizontal shift along the Fairweather and Queen Charlotte Faults, ripping an estimated 1.3 billion cubic feet of rock, ice, and trees from the land and hurling it seaward. As much as 1,300 feet of ice sheared off Lituya Glacier alone. The scars from the earthquake, slide, and tsunami are still visible in the bay today. Cenotaph Island, rising from the middle of Lituya Bay, is still recovering from 1958's great wave, which swept through its midsection, tearing out the forest.

the coast from Harbor Point to observe a Steller sea lion colony on the rocks. Instead, we spot a brownie feeding on a sea lion carcass. Returning to the boat, we motor out of Lituya Bay into a glassy, calm sea and follow the coastline, discovering that the bear is a huge sow with 3 small cubs feeding. Beyond, nearly 100 sea lions lie hauled out on rock islets, seemingly oblivious of the bears. Later, we look for a base camp site. On Cenotaph Island, the bears have beat us to a particularly choice spot. Herbaceous meadows have been munched on, slept on, and uprooted;

cottonwoods are clawed and stripped of bark, some knocked over, and bear trails and scat are ubiquitous. We head to the opposite side of the island, where rangers have camped in past years. Even this beach has bear tracks. I hope they respect our space; there's just nowhere to go where the bears haven't been.

Isolated from the rest of the park by the Fairweather Range of the St. Elias Mountains, the 125-mile-long outer coast is a ribbon of low-lying land with miles of rocky cliffs, sandy beaches, glacial runoff rivers, and a dense band of timbered lowlands pierced by glaciers that push out into the Pacific. The Fairweather Mountains form a barrier, catching precipitation and feeding glaciers, as they thrust up practically from the sea. So close are these spectacular peaks to the ocean shores that they are etched in the memory of anyone who has traveled between Cape Spencer and Dry Bay on a clear day. The early Natives called Mount Fairweather *Tsalxaan*, the Paddler's Mountain. Rising 15,320 feet, its appearance offered the promise of calm seas or warned of storms when cirrus clouds draped its summit.

Between Lituya and Dry Bay lies unbroken wave-beaten coast made up of sand and gravel left behind by the great glaciers, with swift glacial streams pouring into the sea. A tall, narrow band of near-impenetrable forest spreads inland from the coast, some of it clinging to old moraines and beach ridges, some of it growing up on a higher bench of land, having escaped the Little Ice Age. When glaciers flowed down through the valleys between the mountains during the last ice age, short sections of coastal plain in the lee of the high mountains escaped burial by ice, and the land became a refugium. In these small pockets, an 8,000-year-old forest fringe of Sitka spruce, western hemlock, mountain hemlock, and occasional yellow cedar shades shrubs such as menziesia, mountain ash, elderberry, salmonberry, and blueberry, as well as smaller forest plants such as dwarf dogwood, coral-root, single delight, and twisted stalk. Acidic bogs thousands of years old support a variety of species. Padded with moss, lichens, and sedges, they are also home to such plants as the showy but odorous skunk cabbage, carnivorous sundew, pungent Labrador tea, and tiny, single-berried

bog cranberry, and the colorful blossoms of such tiny flowers as bog laurel, bog orchid, yellow lousewort, and ladies' tresses.

▲ AN OUTWASH STREAM FROM FINGER GLACIER MEETS THE GULF OF ALASKA.

Punctuating the forest and linking mountains to sea, great ice fields descend from the Fairweathers to form vast plateau glaciers: Finger, LaPerouse, Fairweather, and Grand Plateau. Only LaPerouse flows directly into tidewater. The others have shrunk back up into their valleys, leaving behind desolate moraines with surfaces that are being reclaimed by forest despite the presence of ice underneath.

Ancient bear trails wind in and out of the forest and along bluffs, deep footprints worn into the earth. Wolves roam on beaches and play in alpine meadows. Seals and sea lions perch on rocks near the entrance to Lituya Bay. Cliffs on Cenotaph Island support rookeries of black-legged kittiwakes, glaucous-winged and Bonaparte's gulls, horned and tufted puffins, rhinoceros auklets, and pelagic cormorants. Rare is the traveler to the coast who isn't humbled by the sheer abundance of wildlife along this narrow strip of coast and offshore waters.

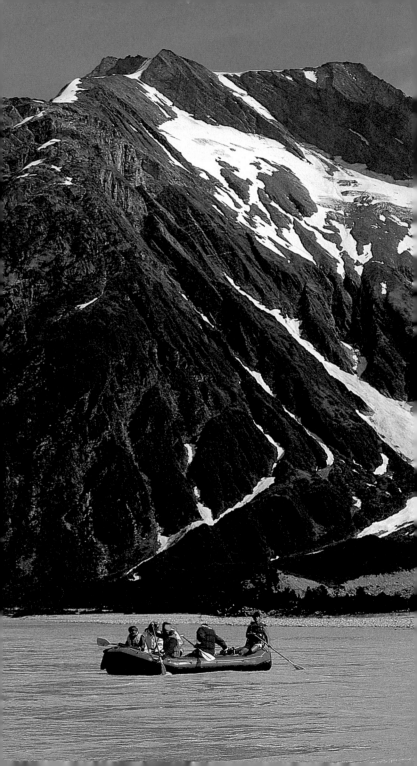

THE TATSHENSHINI
AND ALSEK RIVERS
AND GLACIER BAY
NATIONAL PRESERVE

More than 100 years ago, a seasoned Alaskan outfitter and an English explorer teamed up with two Native guides for the first recorded descent of the Tatshenshini and Alsek Rivers by non-Natives. Jack Dalton had been in Alaska long enough to figure out that the way to make his fortune was not by prospecting, but by guiding newcomers to the Klondike goldfields. He took parties from Haines to Whitehorse over a Tlingit trail he "rediscovered," putting people up at his rustic lodgings on the Tatshenshini River along the way. Edward James Glave, a young Englishman fresh from explorations on the Congo River, had been appointed leader of an 1890 Alaskan expedition sponsored by *Leslie's Illustrated Newspaper* in New York. Glave, a writer with a "keen fascination in traveling through unknown lands," hired Dalton to be his guide for a trip down the Tatshenshini. Piling their gear into a 20-foot-long dugout canoe, Glave and Dalton set out in the hands of Shank, a medicine man, and Koona Ack Sai, who'd made numerous trips down the river. Shooting out into the current, ◄ MOUNTAINS
Glave later wrote for the newspaper, "its forces SOAR ABOVE
. . . combine in one deep torrent which tears RAFTERS ON
along at a bewildering rate, roaring as if THE ALSEK
enraged at its restricted bounds. . . . This RIVER.
stream is the wildest I have ever seen; there is scarcely a 100-yard stretch of fair water anywhere along its course."

Nearly 90 years would pass before the Tatshenshini was again looked on by adventurers seeking white water and wilderness. And today, thousands descend a river whose valley traverses one of the the most remote and wild corners of North America, a place where there was, Glave wrote, "such an incessant display of scenic wild grandeur that it became tiresome." In 1980, with passage of the Alaska National Interest Lands Conservation Act, the U.S. portion of the Alsek River and its surrounding mountains and forelands added 585,000 acres to Glacier Bay National Park, including 55,000 acres of national preserve lands at Dry Bay. Linking vital international wildlands together, the Tatshenshini–Alsek River Valley is an important migration route for plants, fish, and wildlife, home to brown (grizzly) and black bears, moose, snowshoe hares, lynx, wolves, golden and bald eagles, mountain goats, and British Columbia's only winter range for Dall sheep. King, sockeye, and coho salmon, and their cousins the steelhead and Dolly Varden char, migrate upriver to spawning grounds in which they were born.

As we drop our raft into a small, salmon-choked river off the Haines Highway in Canada's Yukon Territory, my friends Ted Handwerk and Ron Beck marvel that these humble headwaters become the mighty, glacially carved Tatshenshini–Alsek River. Ten days and 120 miles from here, the Alsek's flow will be 5 times that of the Colorado River. Even after floating the river 5 times, I haven't tired of the scenery: dancing rapids, soaring peaks, massive glaciers, grizzlies ambling along shorelines, sandbars imprinted with animal tracks, eagles feasting on spawned-out salmon, fields of wildflowers blanketing riverbanks, and the play of light on an immense landscape combine in primal intensity. Beginning at the toe of glaciers in British Columbia and merging with the Alsek 75 miles down-stream, the Tatshenshini River traverses the largest non-polar glaciated mountain system in the world. Squeezed through canyons where it boils up white, fed by rivu-lets, turbid creeks, and 100-foot-high waterfalls, the Tatshenshini River gains power from glacial tributaries large and small, with names like Silver, Sediments, and Detour, and it grows bigger, wilder, and colder each day.

Picture a ribbon of silver gray water sliced into a

multitude of braids and sprawling across a 4-mile-wide valley lined with glacier-draped peaks. This is the view as we cross the international border from British Columbia and float through the dramatic ice fields of the northwest corner of Glacier Bay National Park. The Tatshenshini and Alsek Rivers form the only waterway linking the Interior to the sea from Cross Sound to the Copper River. Slicing deeply through the St. Elias Range, the current pulls relentlessly toward the sea. With each turn in the river, mountains rise, nameless and numberless.

At times we seem to be floating directly into the mountains, but then the river makes a sharp turn, skirting the edges of soaring peaks and pulling us toward a long valley glacier. We pause to camp among sand dunes at the base of a jumbled terminal moraine. In the alders, we find protection against the wind and coastal storms that sweep through the valley like locomotives. A broad, low glacier beckons us to explore, and we follow it up to a chaotic jumble of jagged seracs.

Back on the river, we bob through wave trains, the silt-laden water hissing against our raft, and take an abrupt turn to the south. With the Brabazon Range rising above us, we round a long spit and enter ice-filled Alsek Lake. In the shadow of Mount Fairweather, we watch house-sized icebergs calve from the 5-mile-wide face of Alsek

▼ A HIKER EXPERIENCES A GRAY DAY AT ALSEK LAKE.

Glacier and row through a surreal landscape of crystalline sculptures. At Gateway Knob the river pours out of Alsek Lake, skirting the Deception Hills and becoming the lower Alsek River. Leaving the mountains and wilderness behind, we meander through coastal lowlands, ending our 120-mile adventure back in civilization, so to speak—a rough airstrip and a small fish processing plant at Dry Bay on Glacier Bay National Preserve lands.

National preserve lands at Dry Bay encompass the lower Alsek River, beaches, and forested coastal plain, with the Deception Hills rising on its southern and eastern borders. Dry Bay is a misnomer, for there is no bay, rather a 12-mile-long river delta fronting the ocean and extending back about 7 miles. The mouth of the Alsek is filled with sandbars, islands, and numerous ever-changing channels, so river runners never venture all the way to the sea. Only experienced locals negotiate the often turbulent breakers at the river's mouth. Sand dunes separate the open ocean from dynamic sloughs and estuaries above the mouths of the Alsek and East Alsek Rivers. These sloughs provide rich habitat for wildlife, waterfowl, shorebirds, and migrating salmon.

The preserve offers a striking contrast to the rest of Glacier Bay National Park, where mountains define the roadless wilderness. Gravel ATV roads and trails spread

INTERNATIONAL HERITAGE

Once threatened by a large-scale international open-pit copper-mining operation in British Columbia that would have destroyed wilderness, wildlife, and water quality, the Tatshenshini–Alsek heartland is now permanently protected. On June 22, 1993, thousands of grassroots environmentalists and the governments of the United States, Yukon Territory, and British Columbia celebrated one of the greatest conservation triumphs of the 20th century: creation of the 2.3-million-acre Tatshenshini–Alsek Wilderness Provincial Park in British Columbia. This designation essentially tied the knot around the last wedge of unprotected land in an outstanding bioregion. Today, 24 million contiguous acres encompassing and surrounding the Tatshenshini watershed form the world's largest international wilderness, including the Yukon Territory's Kluane National Park, British Columbia's Tatshenshini–Alsek Wilderness Provincial Park, Wrangell–St. Elias National Park, Glacier Bay National Park and Preserve, and Tongass National Forest's Yakutat Forelands and Russell Fiord Wilderness. These lands are a priceless legacy.

like a net across the flat plain, linking fishers to rivers, cabins, and commerce. Sport, commercial, and subsistence hunting and fishing activities are permitted here. Cabins and other buildings dot the preserve, and planes as large as DC-3s land on the gravel airstrip to pick up fish from the processing plant on the banks of the lower Alsek River. Despite the development, the preserve is a wild land: bears and coyotes wander at will, and on a sunny day, Mount Fairweather fills the sky with its icy splendor.

GUSTAVUS, GATEWAY TO GLACIER BAY

Ready, set, go!" yells Hank Lentfer, Park Service resource management specialist, and I begin stuffing pilot bread, a hefty 4-inch-diameter saltine-like cracker that is a staple throughout rural Alaska, into my mouth. Thirty of us are gathered in a loose circle amidst the old-time Independence Day festivities in Gustavus, competing to consume a cracker and audibly whistle for the judge in the shortest amount of time. Situated on a broad, sandy, outwash plain left by the ice sheet that once covered Glacier Bay, the small, isolated community of Gustavus is surrounded by a spectacular wilderness setting of glaciers, snowcapped mountains, and marine waters teeming with whales, otters, porpoises, and seals. At the moment, my eyes are closed and oblivious to the spectacular mountain and sea vistas; I am totally focused on the production of saliva. Seconds pass, my mouth working furiously. Finally I swallow once, twice, three times; I wave my hand at Hank, the judge of this contest, and pucker my lips, letting out a weak but audible whistle. "Forty-five seconds!" he yells, and I become the uncontested winner of the pilot bread whistling contest. Earlier this afternoon, there had been a spelling bee, three-legged races, and a tug-of-war. Later, there would be a raw egg toss, wood splitting, and a dozen other contests organized by volunteers, bringing out

◄ FRIENDS IN GUSTAVUS SHARE PIES AT SUMMER GATHERING.

the lively spirit and good cheer of a small, close-knit community.

Long before commercial fishing began around Icy Strait, the Hoonah Tlingit established subsistence camps on a point at the mouth of Glacier Bay known for its abundant berries. The Tlingit erected a ceremonial house and a smokehouse on a nearby river. Several Hoonah Tlingit filed for title to lands on the point under the 1906 Forest Homestead Act, but due to a shortage of surveyors, few claims were conveyed. Around 1914, homesteading fisherpeople took up plows on the point, calling it Strawberry Point, and the area developed into an early agricultural community. Ernest O. Swanson came from Elfin Cove, cleared a few acres and tried his hand at growing vegetables. He left after a few years, but the Abraham Lincoln Parker family arrived in 1917 and stayed. By 1935, the population was 29. Neither the Tlingit nor the homesteaders knew that, in 1879, naturalist and paleontologist William H. Dall had honored the king of Sweden by naming the prominent point at Glacier Bay's mouth, Point Gustavus. Around 1940, residents agreed to name the community Gustavus. The climate was perfect for farming, but distribution of fresh produce was difficult and many a boatload spoiled before arriving at its destination. Others tried raising beef cattle, but the animals quickly overgrazed the meager seasonal pasturage on the Gustavus forelands, and wolves, coyotes, and bears also took their toll on the livestock. Still, a handful of settlers stayed on, diversifying into lumber milling and mining and keeping their hand in salmon trolling.

The U.S. Army constructed an airfield in Gustavus during World War II, as well as a shipping base and POW camp at Excursion Inlet. The airfield was 1 of only 4 in Alaska where B-29 bombers could land and take off. The two 5,700-foot and 5,000-foot runways built in 1942 are now used by everything from Super Cubs to jets. When Glacier Bay National Monument was established in 1925, the Gustavus forelands were included within its boundaries. In 1955, President Dwight D. Eisenhower proclaimed a boundary change, excluding more than 20,000 acres of land and water in Gustavus to allow homesteaders to continue occupying their lands.

A LAND REBOUNDING

Large expanses of flat land are rare in Southeast Alaska, but Gustavus has an abundance of it. The large foreland that you see when you arrive by air is a glacial outwash created during the Little Ice Age. It's also the largest of its kind in Southeast Alaska. In the past 200 years, Gustavus and the lands at the mouth of Glacier Bay have risen 20 feet as a result of glacial rebound. With the tremendous weight of a massive glacier gone, the land is slowly rising. I built my Gustavus cabin in 1980, erecting a rough-cut spruce-framed structure on 3-foot pilings in a forest clearing, while nearly the entire area lay submerged in ankle-deep water. Now the cabin rests on dry land. Today, people are building homes on lands that were marshes or tidal flats 20 years ago. Gustavus continues to rise nearly an inch a year.

Today, Gustavus has about 350 residents. Bordered by national park on three sides and a national forest on the other, the community is literally a gateway to Glacier Bay, situated as it is near the bay's mouth. Glacier Bay (and Gustavus) are accessible only by boat or plane, as there are no roads leading here from elsewhere in Alaska. Visitors who arrive by plane or boat en route to Glacier Bay pass through Gustavus on a 10-mile road from the airport to Bartlett Cove, where they hop aboard boats that tour the park's fjords.

Some visitors come to experience the natural beauty surrounding Gustavus while staying at one of the community's many fine inns and bed-and-breakfasts. Miles of beaches beckon hikers, bird-watchers, and photographers. The offshore waters attract commercial and sport fishers and whale watchers. Dude Creek Critical Crane Habitat Area, adjacent to parklands, offers protection for spring and fall sandhill crane migrations. Visitors seeking a slower pace of life enjoy riding bicycles along wooded roads and hiking by the sea. Residents treasure their quiet community, maintaining gardens and making their living

by fishing, working for the National Park Service, supplying visitor services, making and selling arts and crafts, and working in the local school. Stay long enough and you're bound to get caught up in one of the many traditional gatherings—potlucks, poetry readings, chamber music and old-time fiddle music performances, and contra dancing.

▲ A SMALL BOAT HARBOR IN GUSTAVUS LOOKS OUT TO ICY STRAIT. ▶ GLACIAL STREAMS CARRY MOUNTAINS TO THE SEA.

Two hundred and fifty years ago, ice covered Gustavus. The great rivers of ice that formed Glacier Bay have waxed and waned time and time again over the millennia. While lush rain forests, wildflower meadows, and fish-filled streams surround us at the mouth of Glacier Bay today, we come face to face with the Ice Age just 65 miles up the bay. At Glacier Bay, we are witness to constant change—immense, like a forceful earthquake, or subtle, like the sprouting of a flower in rubble. A fine balance exists between witnessing change and causing it. In our enthusiasm to experience Glacier Bay, may we always be mindful that our presence here is a profound privilege. May we all strive to keep Glacier Bay a wilderness, where "white thunder" is heard in the silence of a fjord, where whales and seals feed unimpeded, where birds find refuge, and where our eyes gaze at immense landscapes unattended by human presence and achievements.

RECOMMENDED READING

Armstrong, Robert H. 1995. *Alaska's Birds: A Guide to Selected Species.* Seattle: Alaska Northwest Books.

———. 1996. *Alaska's Fish: A Guide to Selected Species.* Seattle: Alaska Northwest Books.

Burroughs, John, et al. 1987. *Alaska, the Harriman Expedition, 1899.* Ontario: General Publishing Co. Ltd.

Dauenhauer, Nora Marks, and Richard Dauenhauer, eds. 1987. *Haa Shuka, Our Ancestors: Tlingit Oral Narratives.* Seattle: University of Washington Press and Sealaska Heritage Foundation.

Emmons, George T. Edited and with additions by Frederica de Laguna and biography by Jean Low. 1991. *The Tlingit Indians.* Seattle: University of Washington Press.

Ferguson, Sue A. 1992. *Glaciers of North America.* Golden, Colo.: Fulcrum Publishing Co.

Glave, Edward J. November 8, 1890. *Leslie's Illustrated Newspaper.* New York.

Jettmar, Karen. 1993. *The Alaska River Guide: Canoeing, Kayaking, and Rafting in the Last Frontier.* Seattle: Alaska Northwest Books.

Muir, John. 1915 (1991). *Travels in Alaska.* New York: Penguin Books.

Muir, John. Ed. by L. M. Wolfe. 1977. *John of the Mountains: The Unpublished Journals of John Muir.* Madision: University of Wisconsin Press.

O'Clair, Rita M., Robert H. Armstrong, and Richard Carstensen. 1992. *The Nature of Southeast Alaska: A Guide to Plants, Animals, and Habitats.* Seattle: Alaska Northwest Books.

Pielou, E. C. 1991. *After the Ice Age: The Return of Life to Glaciated North America.* Chicago: University of Chicago Press.

Reid, Harry F. *Glacier Bay Field Journal.* 1892. New York: American Geographical Society.

Schofield, Janice J. 1989. *Discovering Wild Plants: Alaska, Western Canada, the Northwest.* Seattle: Alaska Northwest Books.

Scidmore, Eliza R. 1885. *Alaska, its Southern Coast and the Sitkan Archipelago.* Boston: D. Lathrop & Co.

Smith, Dave. 1994. *Alaska's Mammals: A Guide to Selected Species.* Seattle: Alaska Northwest Books.

Stewart, Frank, ed. 1995. *The Presence of Whales: Contemporary Writings on the Whale.* Seattle: Alaska Northwest Books.

Vancouver, George. 1799. *A Voyage of Discovery to the North Pacific Ocean and Around the World.* London.

INDEX

*Page numbers in **bold** face indicate illustrations.*

Alaska Northwest Books™ is proud to publish another book in its Alaska Pocket Guide series, designed with the curious traveler in mind. Ask for more books in this series at your favorite bookstore, or contact Alaska Northwest Books™.

ALASKA NORTHWEST BOOKS™

An imprint of Graphic Arts Center Publishing Company
P.O. Box 10306, Portland, OR 97210
800-452-3032